LOOK TO GERMANY
-
THE HEART OF EUROPE

by Stanley McClatchie

USM, Inc.
Rapid City, SD USA 2001

United States Library of Congress Cataloging in Publication Data
USM, Inc.
International Standard Book Number (ISBN) 0-910667-26-8

    McClatchie, Stanley

Title: *LOOK TO GERMANY - The Heart of Europe*
          First American Replica Edition

1.   HISTORY, Military, World War II, Nazi Party, Austria, Germany, European
2.   POLITICAL SCIENCE, Nazi Party, Germany, World War II

Printed in Hong Kong
Copyright © 2001 by USM, Inc. All Rights Reserved

PUBLISHER'S DECLARATION

The publisher and distributor of this book, USM, Inc., PO Box 2600, Rapid City, SD 57709-2600 USA, wishes to make clear that this book was published in the United States of America for consumption by Americans who, through tradition and under the protection of the US Constitution and Bill of Rights are guaranteed certain absolute rights to freedom of speech and the press, and all the benefits that such rights imply.

It is the specific intent and desire of the publisher and distributor that this book NOT BE distributed and/or sold in Canada, Australia, Switzerland; countries of the European Union (EU), including but not limited to Austria, Belgium, Denmark, Sweden, France, Germany, Italy, the Netherlands, United Kingdom, etc., which do not have the same tradition, and/or do not provide citizens with a right to freedom of speech, belief and expression, and where the simple act of possessing controversial literature related to World War II history may be severely restricted by law, and may result in a fine, incarceration, or both.

Due to the controversial nature of the content of this book and the potential for misunderstanding portions appearing out of context, the copyright owners expressly forbid reproduction of any part of this book, the reproduction of which may tend to alter the original meaning of the larger portion from which the part was extracted. Excerpts published by others in reviews or in critical works which tend to alter the meaning of the general section from which they were taken, will be treated as violations of the rights of the copyright owners and pursued to the full extent of the law. No part of this book may be reproduced in any form without prior written permission from the copyright owners.

        Publisher's Declaration Copyright © 2001 USM, Inc.

DISTRIBUTED EXCLUSIVELY BY:
USM Incorporated
Post Office Box 2600
Rapid City, SD 57709-2600 USA

LOOK TO GERMANY

-

THE HEART OF EUROPE

A LAND OF OLYMPIC ACHIEVEMENT

"And as for this man, Hitler ... Well, I believe we should all like to take him back to America with us and have him organize things there just as he has done in Germany."

A genuine, hundred per cent American said that to me during the Olympic Games. He belonged to a group from my home city, Los Angeles, which I had accidentally met. And the others nodded silent approval to his remarks as if that was the natural conclusion of everyone.

I also had the opportunity of hearing many other foreign visitors express their opinion. Among them were naturally some who were less voluble in their enthusiasm, but the great majority were overwhelmed with admiration for the incomparable Reich Sport Field, the boundless enthusiasm of the German nation for sport, its sincere veneration of the Führer, the spontaneous applause on the appearance of foreign flags, the generous hospitality of the German people, the enviable prosperity evident everywhere in the Third Reich ... in fact, everything.

Somehow, all they saw, heard and experienced did not fit in with the picture of a land of oppression and persecution such as the foreign press reports had led them to expect.

It was certainly the French who experienced the greatest astonishment. As the French athletes marched into the Stadium on the opening day of the Games they obligingly raised their right arm in a salute to the Führer. From that moment on their entry was a triumphal procession. The whole Stadium reverberated with enthusiasm. It seemed as if Paris must have heard those cheers. Finally, after years of war and misunderstanding, the Germans had an opportunity of demonstrating their true personal feelings towards their western neighbours. It was like a revelation.

This is the spirit and attitude in "Fascist" Germany.

One of the "eternal sceptics", a journalist from Paris, opinioned: "It would naturally appear at its best during an Olympic Festival, but what about behind the scenes — the oppressed people ...?" And he shook his head doubtfully.

I had the pleasure of conducting several of my countrymen "behind the scenes". We went one evening to the "Strength through Joy" City, into the midst of the pulsating life of the people. Here we finally succeeded in finding table space in the gigantic Berlin hall, and were regaled with an entertainment such as has never been known in a cabaret or theatrical revue. Opera singers, ballet dancers, revue presentations ... and at the end the entire audience joined in singing. But such singing it was! Completely unrestrained, while everyone stood up, joined arms and swayed back and forth in rhythm. What enthusiasm!

TRIUMPHAL PROCESSION OF THE FRENCH ATHLETES IN THE OLYMPIC STADIUM

In the midst of his countrymen, not far from our table, sat Dr. Ley, and I was able to explain to my companions: "That is the leader of the German Labour Front. All of this which we are enjoying at present is not just for strangers but for the German workers. We are in a Socialistic country. What do you suppose such an entertainment would cost back in America?"

They estimated five to ten dollars.

Then I could inform them: "It costs the German worker no more than a glass of beer. For fifty pfennigs he can even sit in the best seats at the opera and enjoy a vacation on the Baltic for a couple of marks a day."

Afterwards I told them about the Reich Motor Highways, the most magnificent system of thoroughfares in the world; the Hitler Youth, the independently organized and directed organization of the German youth; the Land Year for the school children; the Labour Service; the great national community; the principle of leadership; the successful endeavours to provide employment for all of the workers (America is still burdened with 10 to 12 million unemployed); the trebling of construction work and increase of automobile production to six times its former level; the magnificent German aviation service which encircles the globe, etc. My companions could scarcely believe their ears, but neither could I believe mine when I first entered the Third Reich just twelve months earlier.

UP WITH THE FLAGS OF THE VICTORS AND EVERY HAND RAISED IN SALUTE!

I had, incidentally, lived a number of years in Germany before the rise of National Socialism, and in fact had conducted the first radio broadcasts between Germany and America, among them, a Christmas programme in which leading statesmen expressed Germany's greetings to the American people. Therefore, I feel justified in stating that I am well acquainted with conditions in Germany.

I was compelled, however, to follow the development of the Third Reich through the American press — the most unfavourable channel imaginable. So it was with mixed feelings that I returned to the New Germany.

Then I realized the true extent of the revival and perceived the surging spirit of the German people, who had become so dear to me. It was like a revelation.

Once comprehended, however, the many developments in the Third Reich are taken for granted and no longer give rise to astonishment — until one is himself able to experience the surprise of newly arrived visitors, as in the case of my Olympic companions. Then one suddenly realizes anew that the advancement under Adolf Hitler has been truly phenomenal.

This fact was most conclusively proved in the Olympic Games themselves. Down-trodden, poverty-stricken Germany of 1932 was able to win only three gold medals, while the re-awakened Reich of 1936 emerged from the Olympic combat with thirty-three!

IN BERLIN A FESTIVAL OF RECONCILIATION IS CELEBRATED . . . .

This book will attempt to reveal the Olympian achievements of the New Germany in every field, and just as the German Olympic Bell intoned its appeal:

"I call the youth of the world!"

so is this book intended for young and old in every continent.

The German people are youthful in nature, and only those who are young at heart can truly understand and appreciate the great revival. Only those who share this spirit can comprehend the enthusiasm which inspired these pages.

It is a foregone conclusion that many "sceptics" will regard this work merely as official propaganda, and I have even resigned myself to the idea of being considered the invention of the German Propaganda Ministry. As a matter of fact, the creation of this book is due principally to my good friend and collaborator, Atto Retti-Marsani, who is an Italian, while I myself am descended of a Scotch-American pioneer family. It was not until my work was practically completed that an official department offered me assistance — and this was the Reich Youth Headquarters.

In spite of all that I may say, however, this work will undoubtedly be classed as "propaganda", a fact which I have no intention of denying. It is true that I have aligned myself with the exponents of a definite political philosophy — that of the open hand ...

. . . . .WHILE IN MADRID THE CLINCHED FIST IS RAISED

Today the world stands before a momentous decision: the threatening, closed fist of unbounded **Communism** — or the open raised hand of National Socialism. France and Spain are now at the crossroads. And tomorrow? Every nation must sooner or later answer "Yes" or "No" to all-devouring Communism.

In any case, the world is becoming more socialistic, and it is merely a question of whether the socializing process will involve bloody class struggles, the decimating of the "bourgeoisie", or whether it will proceed quietly and peacefully in the manner of national-socializing, based upon social development and the foundation of national and Christian tradition.

Germany offers an incomparable example of the latter method, and the following pages will endeavour to reveal the progress of this attempt, which is of such vital significance to the present-day world.

> We toil and weave
> Life's burden to carry,
> And struggle courageously forward.
> Brother, my brother, strive on!
>
> Thus we are called,
> Nameless our ranks;
> Tis we who pave the way to eternity:
> Nation of workers, strive on!

SUCH IS THE NEW GERMANY!

Stanley McClatchie

Berlin, February, 1937

HEIL HITLER!

ADOLF HITLER

born April 20th, 1889

HERR

HITLER,

CUSTOMS

INSPECTOR

"Wh — a—t? You wish to become a painter? ... an artist?"

The father was speechless. He had always taken it for granted that his son would one day become an official like himself, who through persistence and diligence had risen from his peasant origin to a position in the service of His Majesty, the King and Emperor.

"Painter? Never, as long as I live! You know the career I have planned for you."

"An official? Never, as long as I live!" blurted out the 12-year old youth stubbornly.

The quarrel continued for almost two years. Then one day the father suffered a sudden stroke which proved fatal. His son, however, did become an official — the first official of the German Reich.

HITLER'S MOTHER

Following the death of his father, the schoolboy, Adolf Hitler, was left to the care of his mother, and under her guardianship he painted to his heart's desire. But his fortune soon changed because within four years she followed his father.

Then the orphaned youth migrated to the metropolis, Vienna; not to the scintillating city of the beautiful blue Danube, however, but to the Vienna of factories, slum dwellings and misery. The newborn proletarian became a construction workman.

On the scaffolding he was forced to listen to the Communistic and Socialistic harangues of his comrades, the principal theme being the "Class Struggle". Some instinct in him, however, arose in opposition to these theories.

In the ensuing argument he became acquainted with an important Marxist maxim: "Knock him down!"

But in spite of this he continued to mount the scaffolding ... and he did become a Socialist.

Next to sketching, the schoolboy, Adolf, loved history. He enjoyed reading about the great deeds of famous men — above all about Chancellor Bismarck and his creation of the German Reich.

In Vienna, following a hard day's work, he continued this habit. But now he had to cope with two worlds: the bourgeois-national, from which he was descended, and the proletarian-Communistic, in which he found himself at that time. The one was influenced by capitalistic exploitation, it is true, but the other was deadly class hatred.

On both sides were German people, however, and here lay the solution: Instead of mercenary profiteering and class warfare, a people's community! Thus there arose in the heart of the young bourgeois-proletarian the national-socialistic span of the abyss which divided the people into two hostile camps.

His highest ambition was to become an architect in the metropolis, but he little dreamt that one day he would build a gigantic bridge—the bridge between two worlds.

AUGUST 2ND, 1914. STORM OVER EUROPE

Suspense reigned supreme in every town and village. Excited crowds surged through the streets and squares. In Berlin, they surrounded the royal Palace. The Kaiser appeared on the balcony and proclaimed to the entire world: "They have forced the sword into my hand."

Another similar crowd filled the Odeons Square in Munich. They shouted, sang and demonstrated... and in their midst was one who was named Adolf Hitler. A press photographer accidentally caught the expression of enthusiasm on his face at that moment. He had been living in Munich for two years—no longer as a construction worker, however, but as a draughtsman. His first period of struggle was over.

Then began the second and more significant conflict. Being the enthusiastic patriot that he was, Hitler volunteered immediately for military service under the King of Bavaria and the German Kaiser. In a few months he received his baptism of fire.

WORLD WAR

A sketch made by Adolf Hitler at the front in 1915

AN UNKNOWN SOLDIER

If voluntary despatch carriers were requested, Hitler was always on hand — from that time on the carrier of a message!

This should not be taken as a foregone conclusion, however. Heroes are not born but forged in the flames of experience. For some time Hitler struggled to overcome the terror of death, five citations for bravery bearing witness to the fact that he also emerged successful in this combat.

He was seriously wounded on two occasions, and, temporarily blinded by mustard gas, he lay in the field hospital on the day that the Armistice was signed.

Then a chaplain approached his bedside and with tears in his eyes told him of Germany's humiliation.

Four years in vain ...

An entire nation bowed before the victorious powers, steeped itself in the grey humdrum of daily existence ... and sought only to forget.

One, however, an unknown soldier, remained unvanquished and was determined to carry on the struggle for the Fatherland to a more successful conclusion.

Ich verzichte hierdutch für alle Zukunft auf die Rechte an der Krone Preussen und die damit verbundenen Rechte an der deutschen Kaiserkrone.

Zugleich entbinde ich alle Beamten des Deutschen Reiches und Preussens sowie alle Offiziere, Unteroffiziere und Mannschaften der Marine, des Preussischen Heeres und der Truppen der Bundeskontingente des Treueides, den sie Mir als ihrem Kaiser, König und Obersten Befehlshaber geleistet haben. Ich erwarte von ihnen, dass sie bis zur Neuordnung des Deutschen Reichs den Inhabern der tatsächlichen Gewalt in Deutschland helfen, das Deutsche Volk gegen die drohenden Gefahren der Anarchie, der Hungersnot und der Fremdherrschaft zu schützen.

Urkundlich unter Unserer Höchsteigenhändigen Unterschrift und beigedruckten Kaiserlichen Insiegel.

Gegeben Amerongen, den 28. November 1918.

RENOUNCEMENT

A significant historical document in which the former German Kaiser renounced his rights to the crown, leaving the nation without a leader and without a government.

An entire nation renounced —
under „the threatening danger of

ANARCHY, STARVATION and FOREIGN DOMINION!"

..................................ANARCHY..................................

German War Children Fed by the Quakers

STARVATION

The Watch on the Rhine

. . . . FOREIGN DOMINION . . . .

THE UNKNOWN SOLDIER DEFIES A WORLD OF ENEMIES ....

Beyond the frontiers, the foreign powers insisting upon the fulfilment of the debasing Treaty of Versailles; at home, the Marxists carrying on their agitation for class disintegration!

One against all! Thus the unknown corporal, Adolf Hitler, began his campaign, with words as his only weapons. He did not speak until ten months after the Armistice, and then only before a tiny group in Munich. He stood up with uncertainty, but as he spoke a slumbering fire awoke in his breast. It smouldered and broke into flames. From that moment he was no longer a nameless individual, but the fiery orator of the people, and he set out to conquer an entire nation.

"Comrades, unite!" rang out his message. "Unite and cast aside the foreign yoke! Unite and strive together for the welfare of Germany."

.... AND THOUSANDS OF COMRADES THRONG INSPIRED TO HIS SIDE!

From dozens his followers became hundreds, and before long thousands had responded to his call. Within a year the new leader of the people was filling the largest halls in Munich.

Beginning with a group of seven men, he created a party of millions and called it National-Socialist — a daring union of two words which had formerly represented radically opposite concepts. He called his movement the German Workers' Party, since every citizen should become a worker and toil for the welfare of the national community.

Adolf Hitler then devised a flag for his party — an extremely remarkable banner, since it was blood red like that of his Marxist opponents. But in the centre of the field was a white circle, and in the midst of this a swastika, an ancient symbol of the sun signifying the reviving source of all terrestrial forces of life.

"S.A. MARCHES" — HORST WESSEL AT THE HEAD OF THE COLUMN

"With a handful of resolute war comrades I formed a group during the years, '19 and '20, for protecting the assemblies of our movement. Reckless dare-devils they were, who had no fear of numbers or threating danger. Since our struggle was at first limited to the conquest of assembly halls, their duties were somewhat limited. In a violent battle for the possession of a hall in 1920, the first major combat of the new movement, forty-six of these inconquerable patriots asserted themselves against more than 800 opponents. When the battle was over, the main hall of the Munich Hofbräuhaus resembled a battlefield. Scarcely one of my comrades was without wounds, and their blood-stained hair fell in matted strands over their bruised faces. In one violent assault the red mob was forced out of the hall and the meeting could continue undisturbed.

And as though by magic the young group suddenly became known as the 'Storm Troops'."

Adolf Hitler
in "The Brown Army"

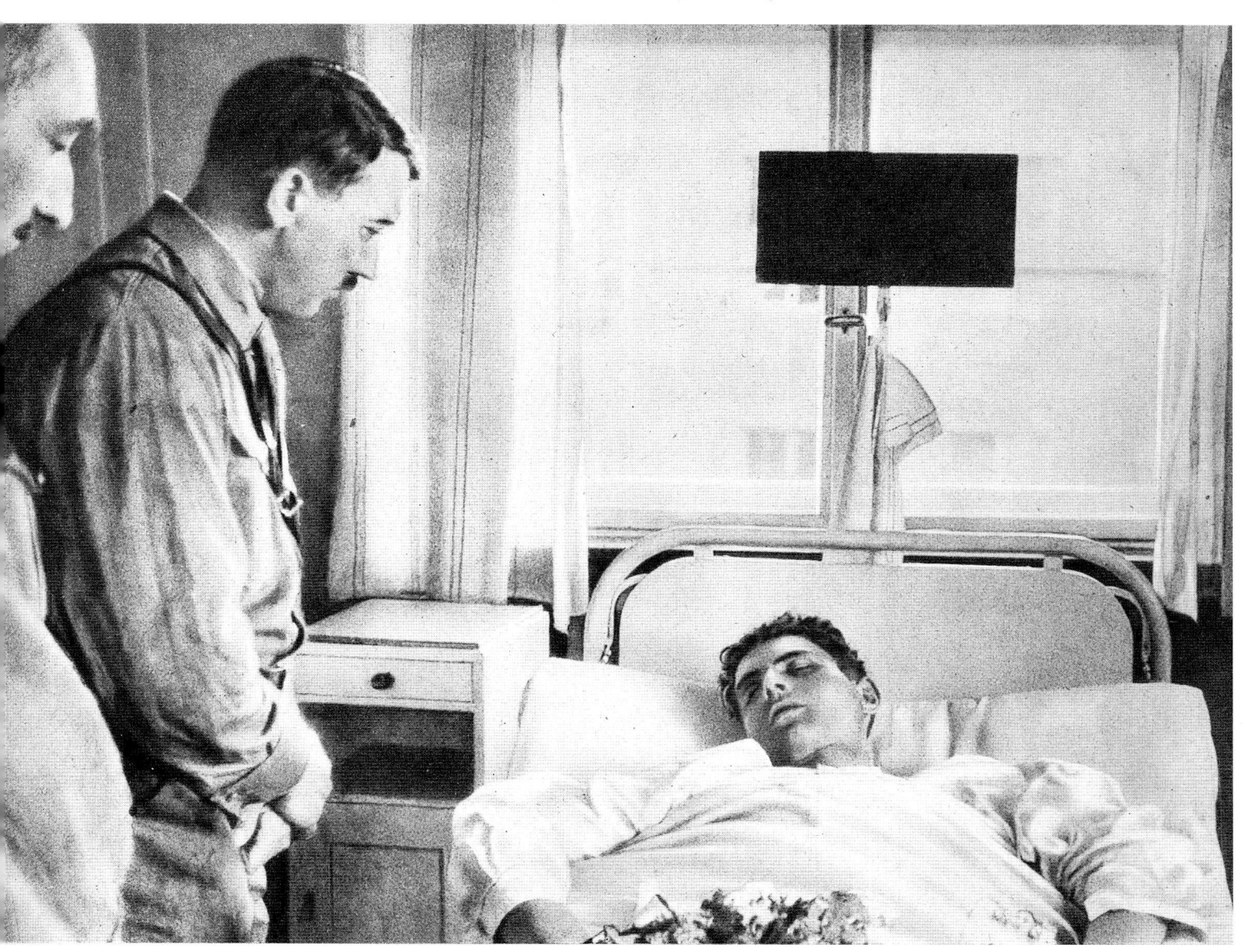

One who gave his life

for his Führer . . . . . .

GERMANY SINKS IN A FLOOD OF PAPER

By 1932 the inconquerable soldier was at the head of the largest political party in Germany. Two hundred and thirty "Brown Shirt" members had been sent by the people to the Reichstag.

Nevertheless, it was still only one amongst thirty-eight parties, and the life and death struggle with Communism had by no means been decided. Disintegrated and divided into countless political factions, the German nation was fighting against itself. The bloody street battles betokened approaching civil war, while even in the Reichstag and National Assembly the representatives engaged in open brawls. And just as bad — in fact more devastating than the inflation — was the flood of words with which Germany was deluged. From thousands of printing presses and hundreds of thousands of platforms surged this uncontrolled avalanche of words — revival through preaching and writing instead of united ACTION. A lack of initiative which at that time was termed "unemployment" threatened to lead the Reich into bankruptcy. The streets were full of beggars, deception and crime became ordinary occurrences, and the oncoming youth deteriorated. The government was helpless, cabinets changed from month to month, and the parliamentarian-capitalistic democracy was on its death-bed.

"THIS CANNOT GO ON!"

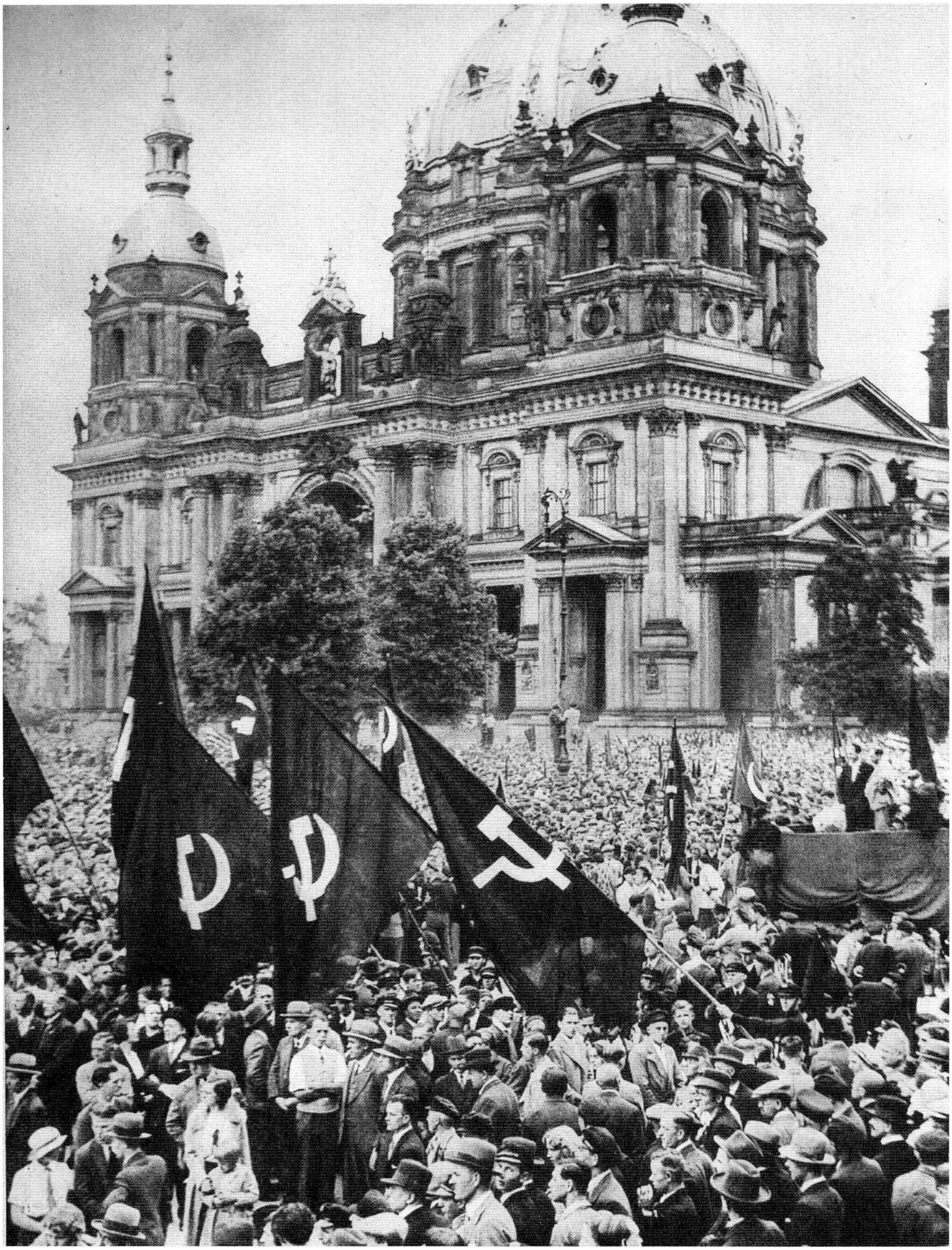

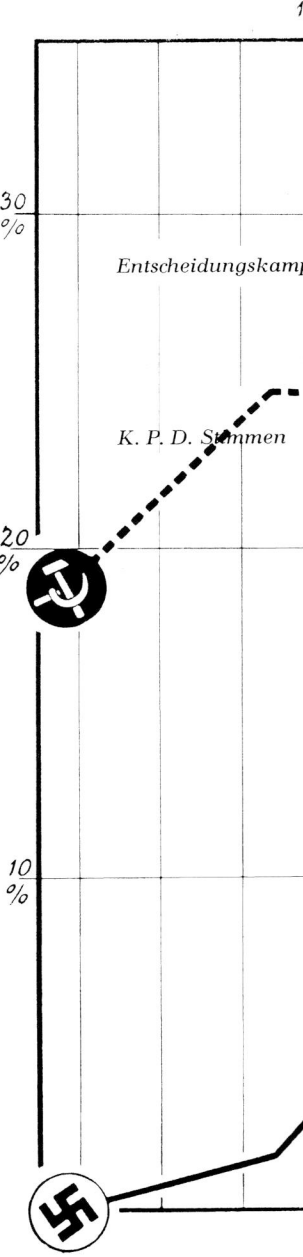

COMPETITION
Election Result

30 %
Entscheidungskamp
K. P. D. Stimmen
20 %
10 %

The helpless central parties

Germany's
Moscow or

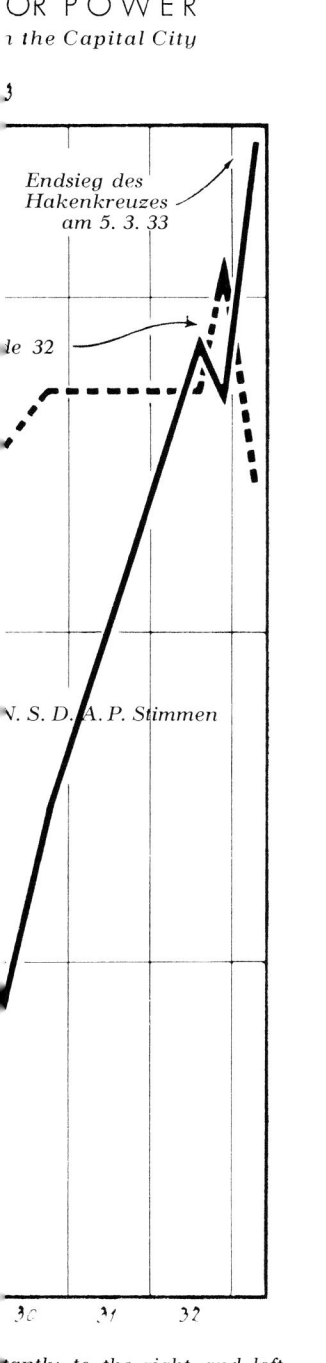

OR POWER
 the Capital City

Endsieg des
Hakenkreuzes
am 5. 3. 33

le 32

N. S. D. A. P. Stimmen

30   31   32

tantly to the right and left

Choice:
Adolf Hitler

The Solution on January 30th, 1933!

UNRESTRAINED ENTHUSIASM

OF THE PEOPLE

Finally a
MAN OF ACTION
again in the

Reich Chancellery

"RECOVERY"

At the beginning of 1930 the two outstanding industrial countries of the world faced chaos. Both had sunk into an economic depression and a third of the working population in each of them was unemployed.

The most threatening aspect of Germany's plight, however, was her political crisis. At the very moment when capitalism was fighting for its life, parliamentarianism went completely bankrupt. In the United States the nervous system of the entire industrial organization ceased to function, and in March, 1933 all of the banks in the land of dollars closed their doors.

On January 30th, 1933 Adolf Hitler took over the helm of a helpless Germany and from that day onwards an astonishing revival began. Within 10 months the industrial employment figures revealed an increase of 25%.

At the beginning of March, in the midst of the bank crisis, Franklin D. Roosevelt assumed the office of President, and an equally astonishing recovery of America's nerve-shattered business began. The people were enthusiastic about their new President.

German enthusiasm for Adolf Hitler increased during the following years, and the Führer won victory after victory in the field of politics, foreign relations and economics. His greatest victory, however, was achieved after three years — the occupation of the Rhineland and the offer of peace to the world. Recognition was not confined to Germany but was shared throughout the world. During the same period of time the President of the United States was forced to defend himself against a storm of criticism. His promising economic measures had long since failed and were even declared unconstitutional by the Supreme Court.

The President of the United States had made business recovery his principal goal, whereas the Führer placed completely "uneconomic" aims in the foreground. His one and only object was the welfare and security of the German nation.

Nevertheless, Germany's economic recovery was much greater, as the curves on the opposite page reveal, and this in a poor country, exhausted by an unsuccessful war and the burden of heavy debts. This can be asserted even in comparison with the richest of all countries in the world where the natural resources are inexhaustible and the gold supply is more than 100 times as great as that in Germany.

What happened to liquidate the initial success of President Roosevelt? According to the opinion in his own country, he alphabetized everything. He instituted a series of measures giving each a name, and these were later designated by the initial letters. The most outstanding of them was the N.R.A., through which it was intended to organize the entire economic life of the country and to regulate and further it through salary and price agreements. A.A.A. was intended to bring salvation to the farmer, etc., etc.

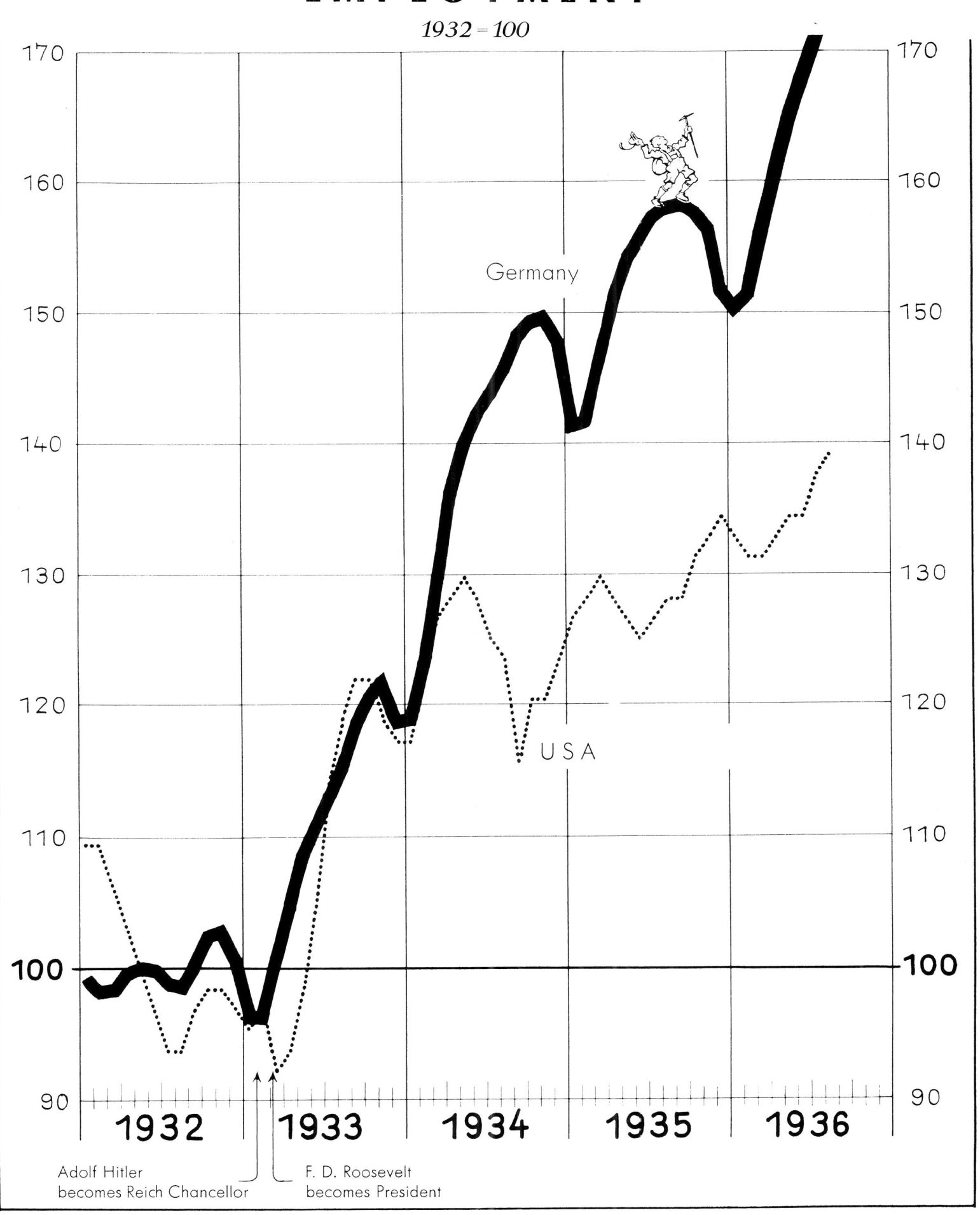

It should not be forgotten, however, that through his dealing with the bank crisis the President was regarded as the saviour of the nation and that people in all walks of life granted him their unconditional confidence. Thus the person of the President became the centre of power in the country. He in turn exercised this leadership entrusted in him as a personal power. In whichever direction he chose to exert his power, success was certain, because there was no outstanding opposition to his will.

Such a dynamic situation made him perforce a "dictator" since the power of a dictator can never be more than that entrusted to him by the people.

In spite of this fact, the mere mention of a "dictator" conjures up a ghost to most "hundred per cent" Americans, and for this reason the bare idea of dictatorship had to be scrupulously avoided. And so it happened that the will and activities of the President were gradually veiled through an alphabetical regiment.

No nation on the earth, however, is willing to relinquish its powers to a mere ideal, a bureaucracy, an alphabetic array. Just as the power of Christianity is concentrated in the person of the Saviour, so the power of the State revolves about the person of the statesman. In short, this is the principle of leadership such as dominates every human group from the family upwards.

During times of prosperity and calm the central leadership of the nation is scarcely evident, but with the approach of a crisis, be it of an economic or political nature, the central unification of forces becomes obviously dominant.

America enjoyed such a concentration of power in the period of her greatest exertion. During his tenure of office, Woodrow Wilson was the most powerful "dictator" in the world, but as soon as the Great War came to an end this unusual concentration of power was again disseminated. Today, however, with 10 million unemployed in the country, such a concentration of power is again essential.

The Germans alone have benefitted by the lesson of the past years of crisis. This is expressed symbolically in the words: "Adolf Hitler is Germany", and every "Heil Hitler" is an acknowledgement of the national leader. Every arm stretches towards him and the forces of the nation are concentrated in his person and distributed through his actions.

This Germany of united will and action has become a power which inspires the world to respectful consideration... or gives rise to fear... or calls forth ridicule and insults.

The more the new Germany is subjected to indignity and opprobrium the less her critics will be able to gain a clear insight into the true state of affairs. An eternal and universal principle is in operation here—the principle of leadership. And the nation which is determined to observe this principle and govern its actions accordingly will certainly one day play a leading role in the history of mankind.

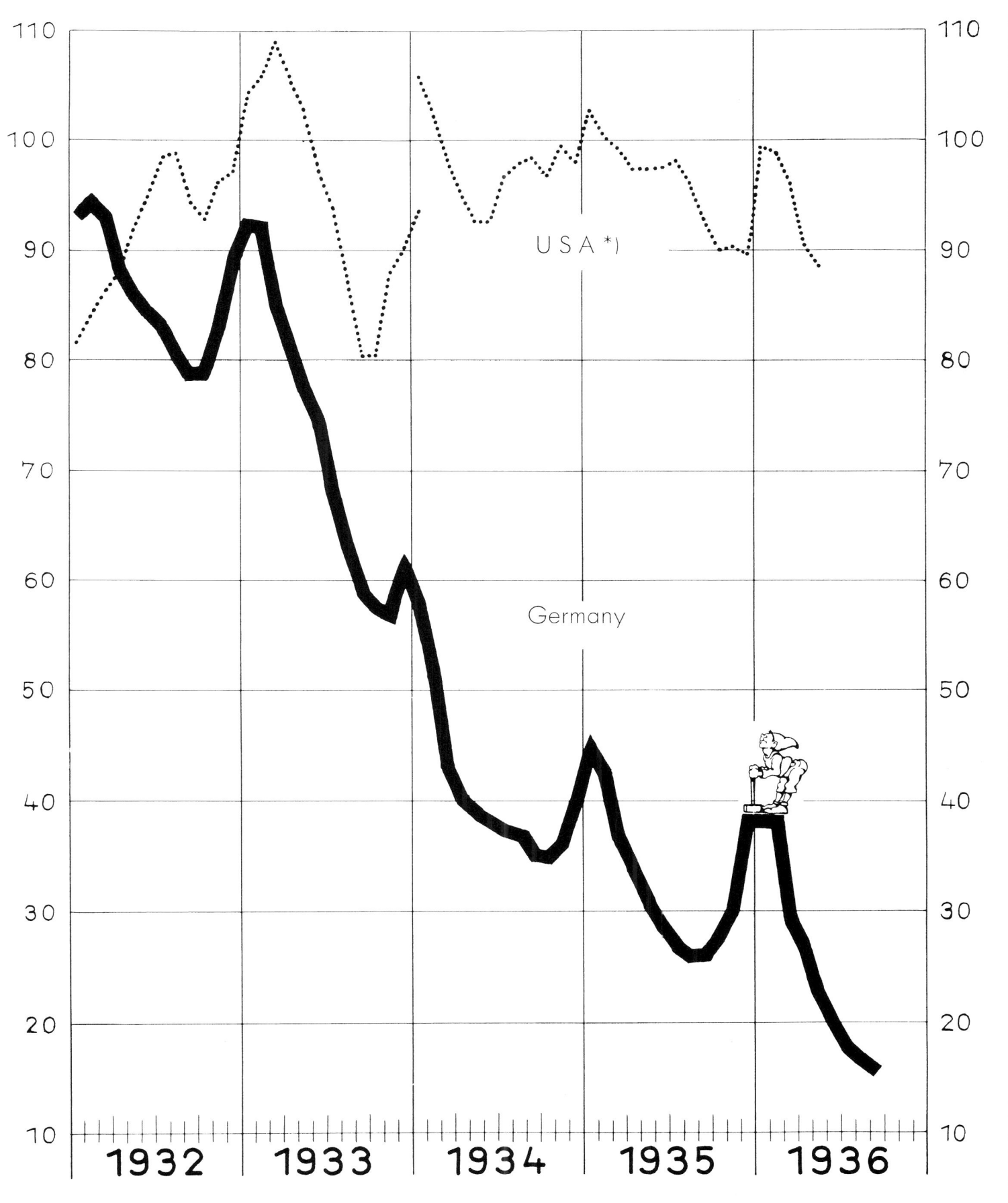

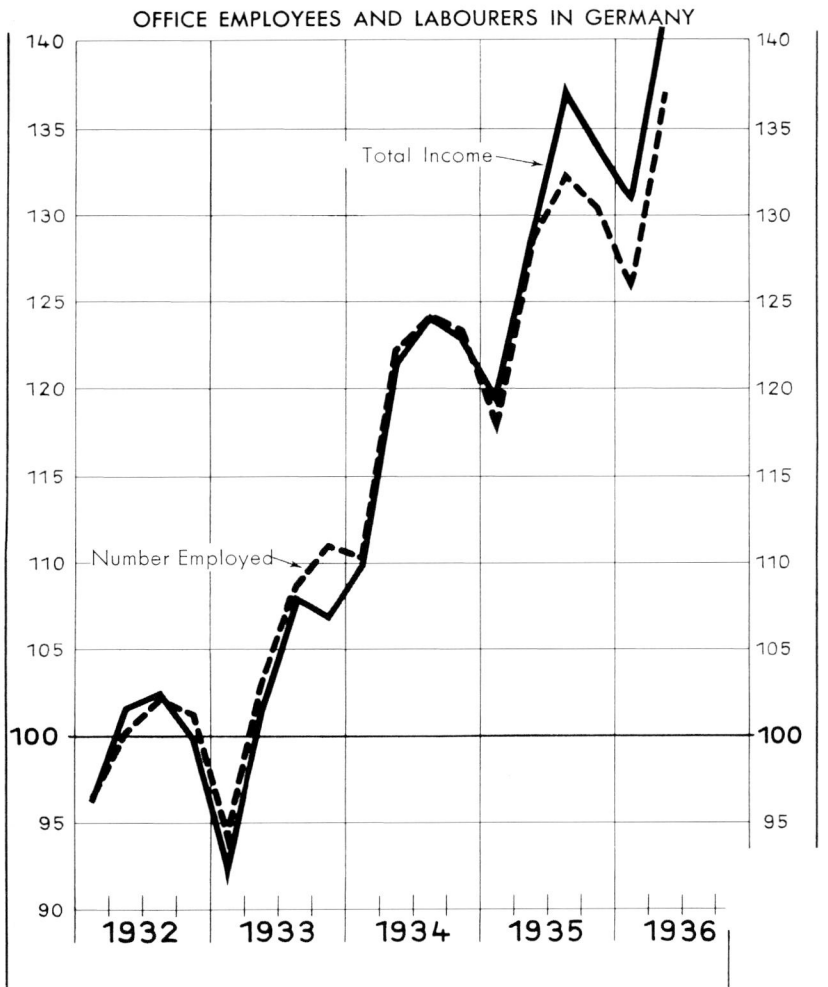
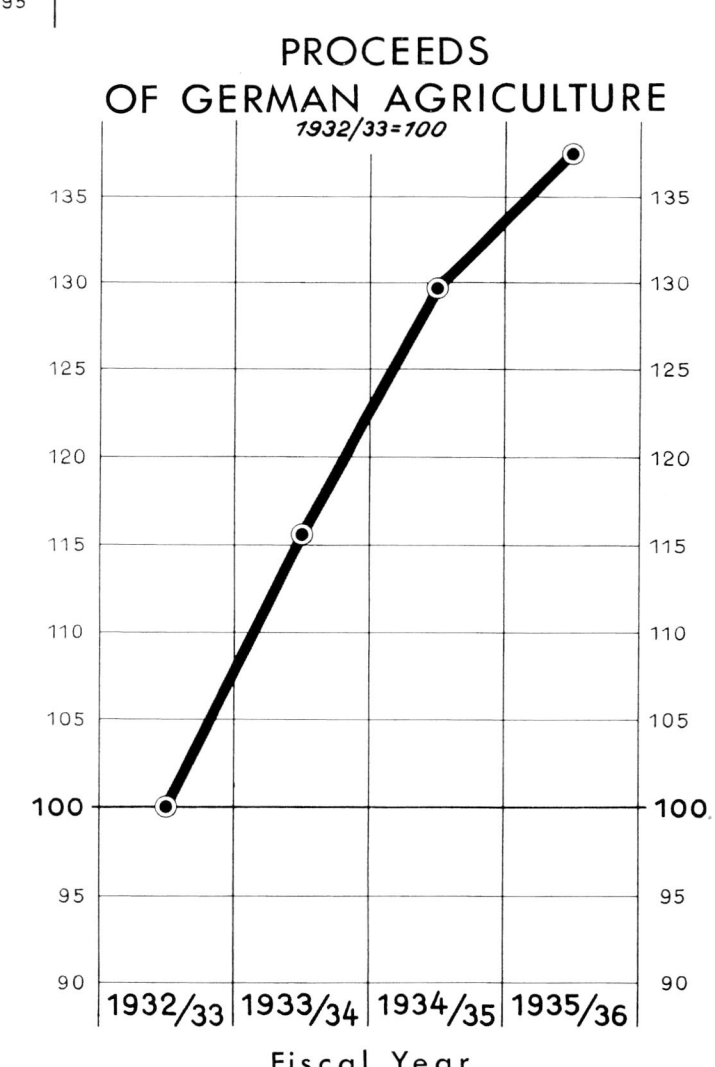

Statistics supplied by
THE INSTITUTE FOR BUSINESS RESEARCH
— Berlin —

THE NATIONAL MOTOR HIGHWAYS

"THE HIGHWAYS....................

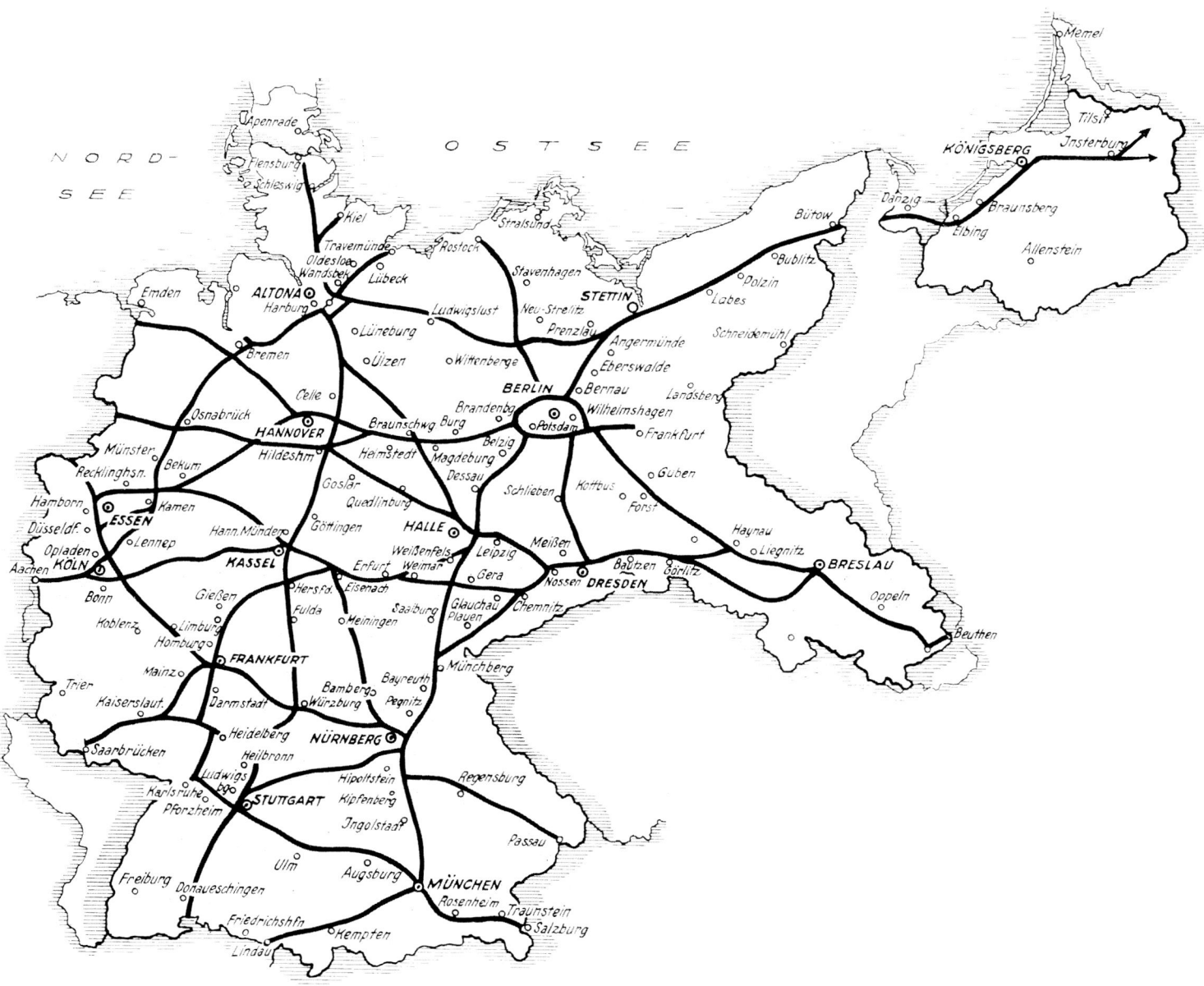

THE LARGEST CONSTRUCTION PROJECT
IN EUROPE! — THE MOST MAGNIFICENT
NETWORK OF HIGHWAYS IN THE WORLD

..................OF ADOLF HITLER"

NO ONE IN THE HISTORY OF MANKIND HAS

UNDERTAKEN A TASK EQUAL TO IT IN SCOPE

GENERATIONS A THOUSAND YEARS HENCE WILL LOOK UPON THE NATIONAL MOTOR HIGHWAYS JUST AS WE TODAY REGARD THE PYRAMIDS, THE ROMAN ROADS AND THE GREAT WALL OF CHINA

The Pyramid of Cheops has always been regarded as the most imposing expression of the will of an individual, but all of the construction achievements of the Pharaohs combined do not equal that of the Führer in his highway construction programme.

The Roman Roads were formerly granted the distinction of being the most extensive network of imperial highways in the world, but in seven years the Third Reich will surpass what the Romans required centuries to complete.

The Great Wall of China is still held to be the most stupendous construction project in the world, but an entire dynasty carried on this task, which lasted several centuries.

The construction achievements involved in the digging of the Suez and even Panama Canal were surpassed by the German highway project in its third year, and by the time it is completed it will have no equal in all of Europe.

THE NATIONAL MOTOR HIGHWAY FOLLOWS ITS OWN ROUTE. IT CONNECTS WITH NO OTHER THOROUGHFARE, PASSES THROUGH NO TOWN OR VILLAGE AND S ENTIRELY FREE OF CROSSINGS

Every crossing is bridged, this involving the construction of about 10,000 bridges.

It is a double highway throughout, containing two roadways each 23 feet wide separated by a 12 foot strip in which grass and shrubbery are planted.

The total length of the National Motor Highways is 4350 miles. Begun in the first year of the Third Reich, they will be completed in the seventh.

During the first three construction years 620 miles of highway were completed, a quarter of a million workers being employed.

The National Motor Highways constitute the first network of roadways in the world which are entirely free of crossings and which avoid all towns and villages. They represent the first carefully planned system of national roadways in the world.

ONE FLIES OVER THE NATIONAL MOTOR HIGHWAYS

When travelling over the National Motor Highways, one has the sensation of unrestrained
FLIGHT.

Up to the present time the motorist has had to give his whole attention to curves, crossings and residential sections, being constantly prepared for every unexpected danger and even having to slow down frequently and stop. On the National Motor Highways, however, he can "step on the gas" with a feeling of perfect security since in front of him lie long stretches of straight roadway or wide, swinging curves, and always before him an
OPEN ROAD.

It is for this reason that a journey over these endless, unobstructed highways reminds one of flying.

In reality, travel on the National Motor Highways is almost as fast as in the air. In the first place, the motorist can accelerate his engine on the open streches, and secondly, an average high speed can be maintained for the entire journey. In fact, an average of 90 miles per hour can be maintained, which borders on aeroplane velocity.

A new type of motorcar must be built, however, for these thoroughfares, so that it can truly be asserted that the National Motor Highways have brought about a revolution in the German automobile industry.

Yesterday America stood at the top of the automobile world. Today Germany has taken her place.

MOTOR HIGHWAY SIGNIFIES FREE THOROUGHFARE

The National Motor Highway is not merely free of crossings, but also of toll.

Free highway! Not only to the private automobile owner but to the entire motoring world. This is its principal mission.

The pioneers in the field of automobile and motor construction were Germans, and such names as Otto, Diesel, Daimler and Benz are renowned throughout the world, but through the Great War and the ensuing burden of taxation the German automobile industry suffered a serious setback. Today only one in every 75 Germans drives a car whereas every fifth American is an experienced motorist.

It is in Germany, which possesses so few automobiles, that this most magnificent highway network in the world is being constructed. A courageous undertaking! But a typical National Socialist enterprise! Just as the individual is unable to flourish without the cooperation of his fellowmen, the automobile industry cannot develop until adequate highways have been constructed. It is for this reason that Germany has undertaken such an immense project, and there is no doubt but that the industry will react to the fullest extent.

The Führer once declared that every industrious citizen should one day drive his own car, and therefore the National Motor Highways are free.

Courageous and undaunted, the Motor Highway follows its course. Crossings, depressions and valleys are resolutely bridged.

Stern but beautiful! Ever-changing but always fitting in with the landscape, the Highway conforms with every district through which it passes.

"CURVE" RHYTHM

The route of the National Motor Highways was always freely chosen and it could have been laid in endless straight stretches. But no! Graceful curves have been built into it so that the motorist will never become tired or fall asleep at the steering-wheel because of the monotony of an undeviating, straight roadway.

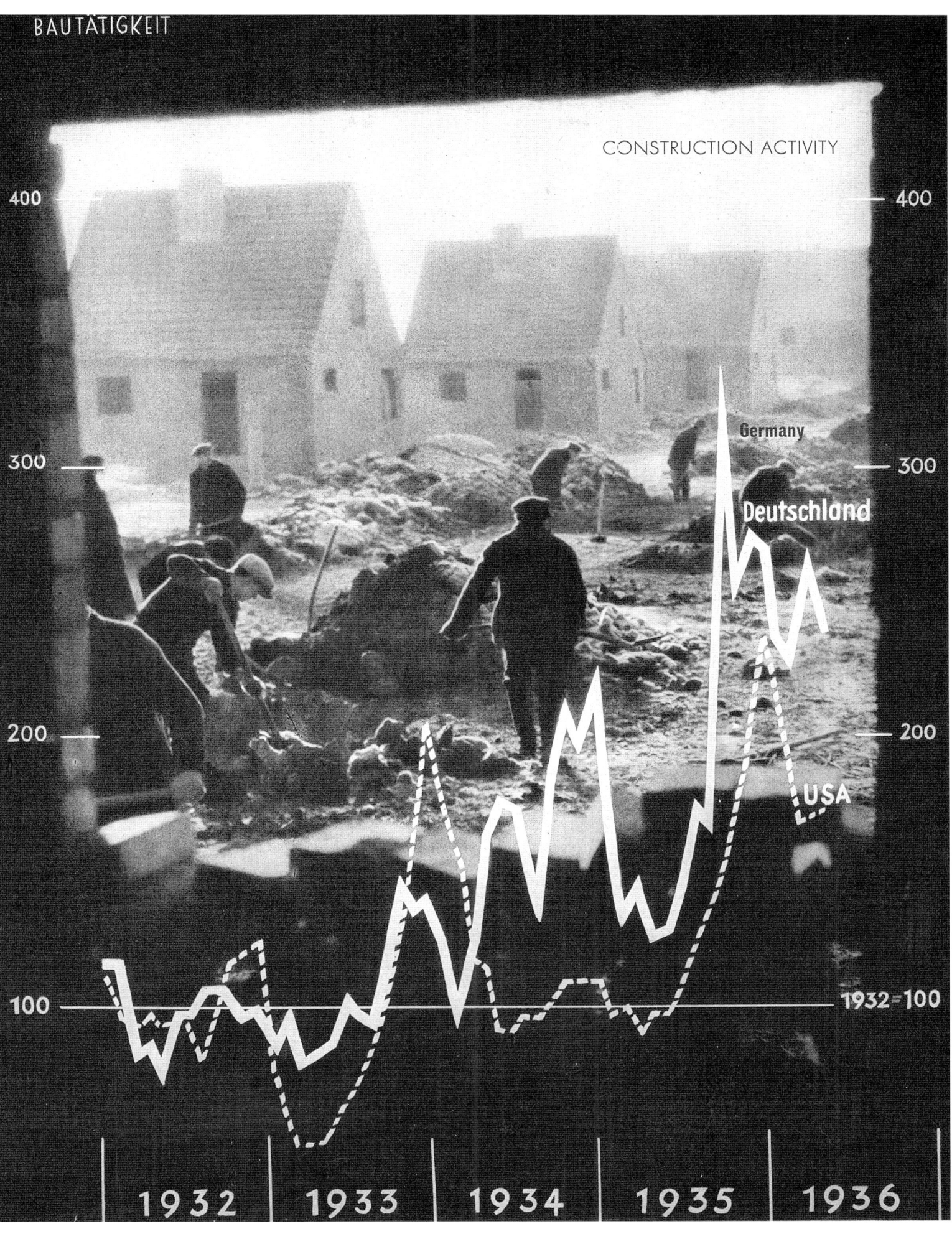

THE FÜHRER HEADQUARTERS AND TEMPLE OF HONOUR IN MUNICH
CREATIONS OF THE ARCHITECT OF THE THIRD REICH

FÜHRERHAUS UND EHRENTEMPEL
IN MÜNCHEN
BAUTEN DES BAUMEISTERS DES DRITTEN REICHES

CITADEL OF THE ORDER AT VOGELSANG

ORDENSBURG VOGELSANG

BUILDING FOR THE FUTURE

In the course of its development one of the prime considerations of the National Socialist Reich was the training of the leaders of the future, and in order to ensure a competent group of leaders for the generations to come three extensive construction projects were undertaken shortly after the rise of National Socialism to power, the "Citadels of the Order" or to use the German word, the "Ordensburgen".

These educational centres are situated far from the ceaseless turmoil of the large cities, and the theories propounded here are in no way connected with the confined academic ideas of the ordinary institutions of learning. No school certificate, no entrance examination and no sum of money will open the doors of these highest educational institutions of the New Reich to a candidate who is unworthy. The youths who are accepted here must exhibit the highest qualities of manhood and have proved their worth in sacrifices for the Party and their fellowmen. Each year one thousand of the most promising candidates are selected from the ranks of the young National Socialists and sent for a year to one of these three institutions. Here they are trained in the principles of self-sacrifice and leadership. Candidates who are married are given preference in the selection.

The director of this project, Reich Organizing Leader, Dr. Ley, has defined the aims as follows:

> "The highest positions in the Party and State are open to every true citizen, regardless of whether he is a labourer, peasant or craftsman, through the medium of these institutions. Never before has the way been open to such possibilities. A truly revolutionary act of unlimited scope!"

Out of the spirit of the past and the inspiring deeds of the patriots of bygone days grows the living spirit of the New Germany. The central edifice among the new buildings in Munich is the Temple of Honour in which the martyrs of the National Socialist Movement are at rest and before which an eternal watch is kept. On the occasion of every large Party demonstration the dead are remembered, and the new National Anthem of Germany recalls those who "march in spirit in our ranks..."

Religion grows from the spirit of piety, and the creative forces responsible for the New Reich are deeply religious in nature. All religion looks upward to the white radiance of eternity and the highest architectural expression of this striving is the Gothic dome. Because of the heavy stone used in its construction this form of expression has never achieved the fullest perfection. Through the means of modern science, however, the newly awakened Germany has fulfilled this primaeval dream of humanity in a superb manner. Hundreds of thousands at the last Nuremberg Party Congress witnessed this fulfilment in breathless silence. A gigantic dome formed of shafts of light suddenly penetrated the darkness, rising into endless space. No photograph could reproduce this overpowering impression; it can only be suggested in a vague manner by the pictures reproduced on the following pages.

On this occasion the members of the Reich Organizing Headquarters took the following vow of faith before the Führer:

"During this consecrated moment when an endless dome rises above us we solemnly vow: We believe in an Almighty God in Heaven who created us, watches over us and directs our actions, and who sent you, our Führer, to free Germany . . ."

Cathedral of Light
Reichs Party Day 1936

Dom des Lichtes
Reichsparteitag 1936

With seating space for 20,000 the D E U T S C H L A N D   H A L L is the largest hall in Europe

In its mass demonstrations National Socialist Germany has broken every world record. The Zeppelin Field in Nuremberg revealed in the night photograph on the previous pages is 90,000 square metres in size and can accommodate 250,000 demonstrators as well as 70,000 spectators. At the present time a new arena five times as large is being constructed.

The home of the Olympic competitors from throughout the world: T H E   O L Y M P I C   V I L L A G E

The largest hall in the world: The new PARTY CONGRESS HALL in Nuremberg (Model)

The new Congress Hall of the Party will accommodate an audience of 70,000, the stage alone seating 5,000. Far from every city stands the Bückeberg, where an assembly ground for one million has been constructed. It is here that the annual Harvest Thanksgiving Festival is held. Almost five million admission tickets were sold for the Olympic Games.

The most magnificent of all sporting facilities: the REICH SPORT FIELD with its stadium constructed of limestone

Remains of a "liberal" epoch

The New Germany provides in this manner for its citizens

A new life begins for parents and children

Such suburban settlements are to be seen in every part of the Reich

"BERGHOF" — The home of the Führer in Obersalzberg, Upper Bavaria

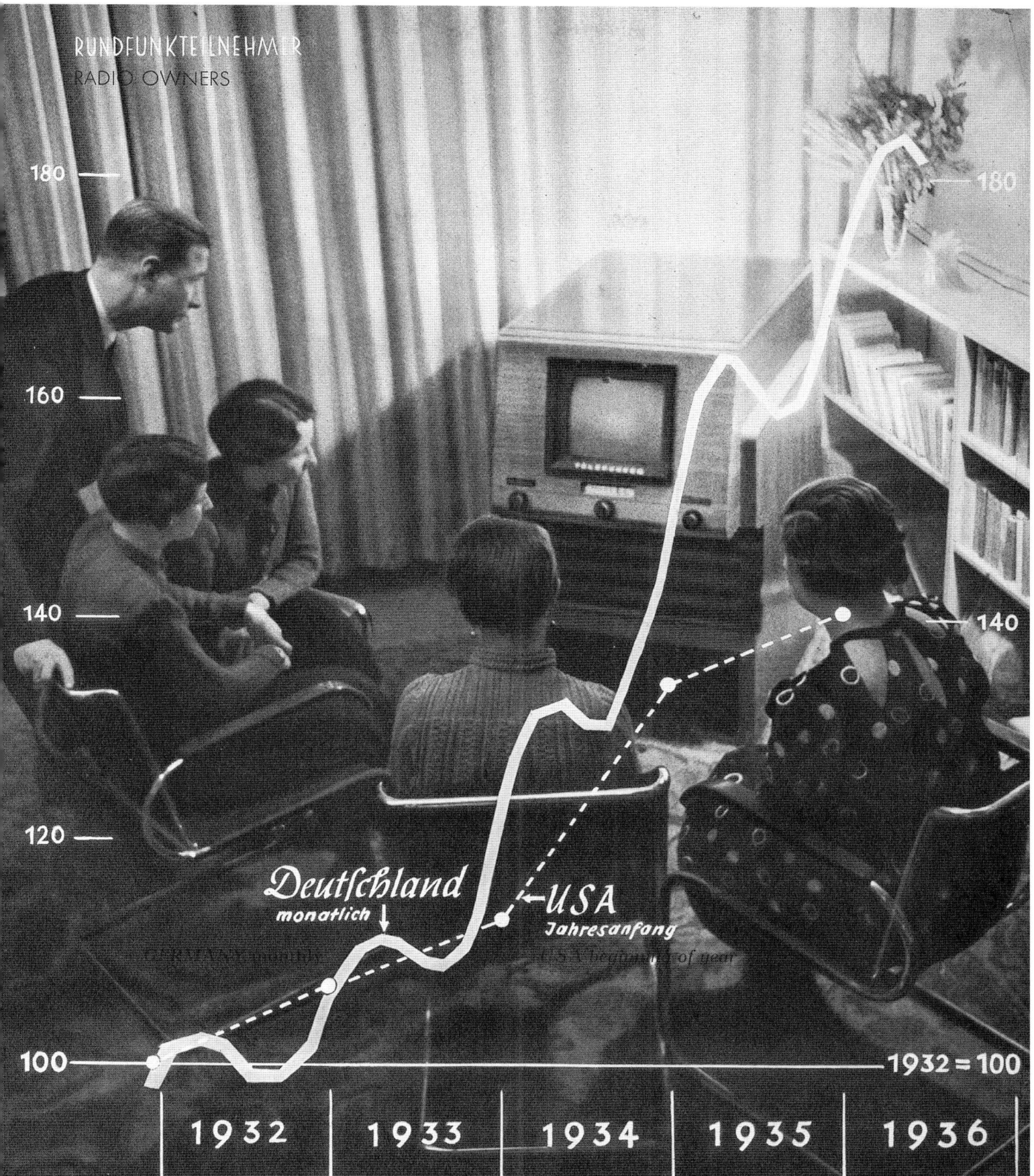

German radio **listeners** are also becoming **televisionists**

On January 30th, 1933 a young Storm Trooper marched into the Berlin Radio Headquarters and informed the surprised personnel that the people of Germany would now listen to their Führer — and they did — that same evenig.

The young patriot was named Hadamowsky, and today he is the director of the Reich Broadcasting Company. He is not content, however, as were his predecessors, to confine his efforts to the office, but can always be found in the heat of activity as shown by the above picture.

The members of the Hitler Youth are also active radio supporters, the one to the left giving his undivided attention to the cutting of a broadcasting record.

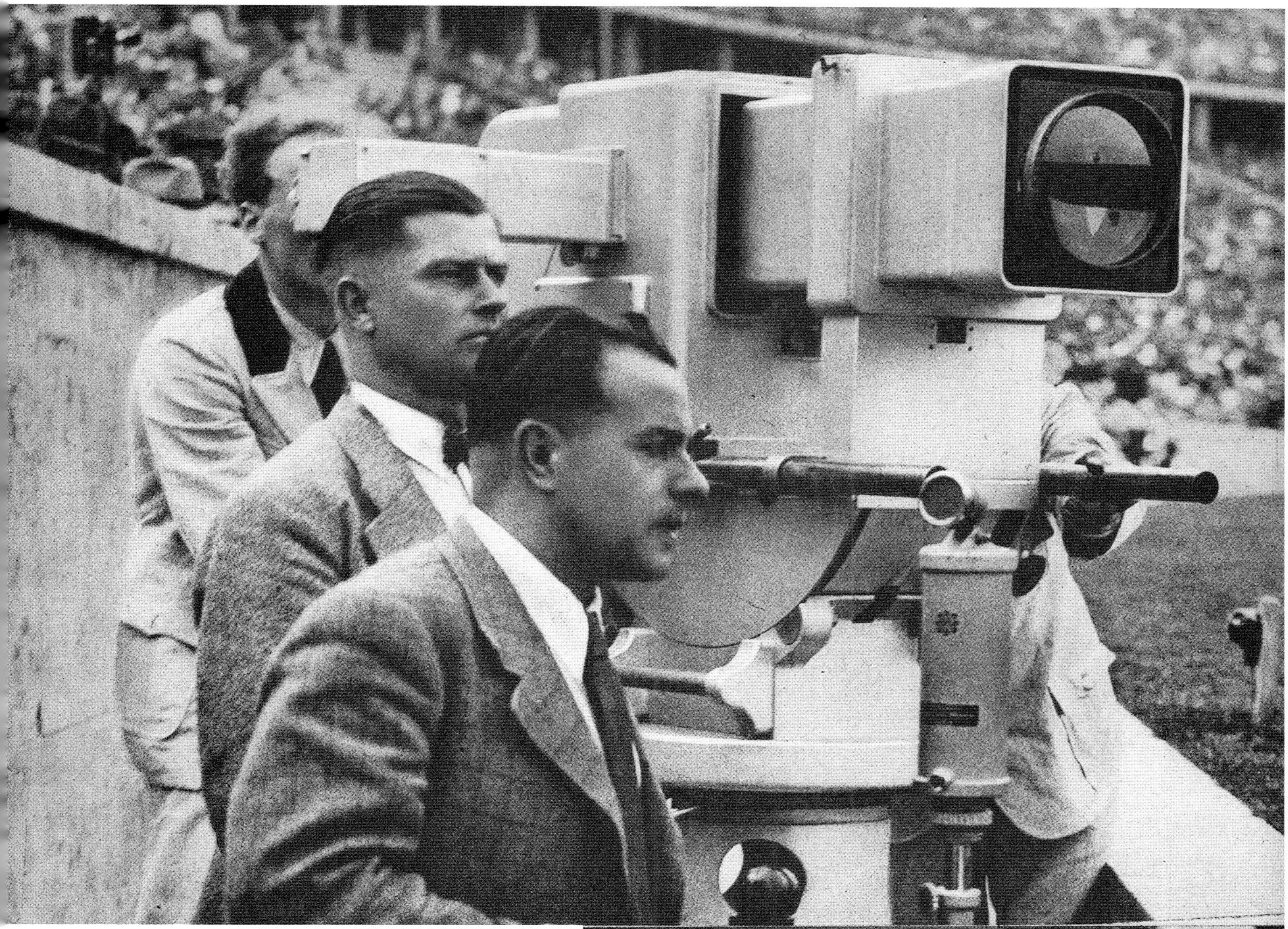

Under National Socialist State leadership Germany has captured the foremost place in the field of radio from America. In television, however, Germany is the pioneer. The entire development in television is based upon the Braun tube invented by Professor Braun and the Nipkow grid of Paul Nipkow. To the right, Herr Nipkow inspects the new broadcasting apparatus which bears his name.

Above: The "Television Cannon" at the Reich Sport Field. The events of this world festival were transmitted for the first time by television, and during the Games public television rooms were open to the German populace free of charge.

Germany has also installed the first television-telephone service in the world.

(see next page)

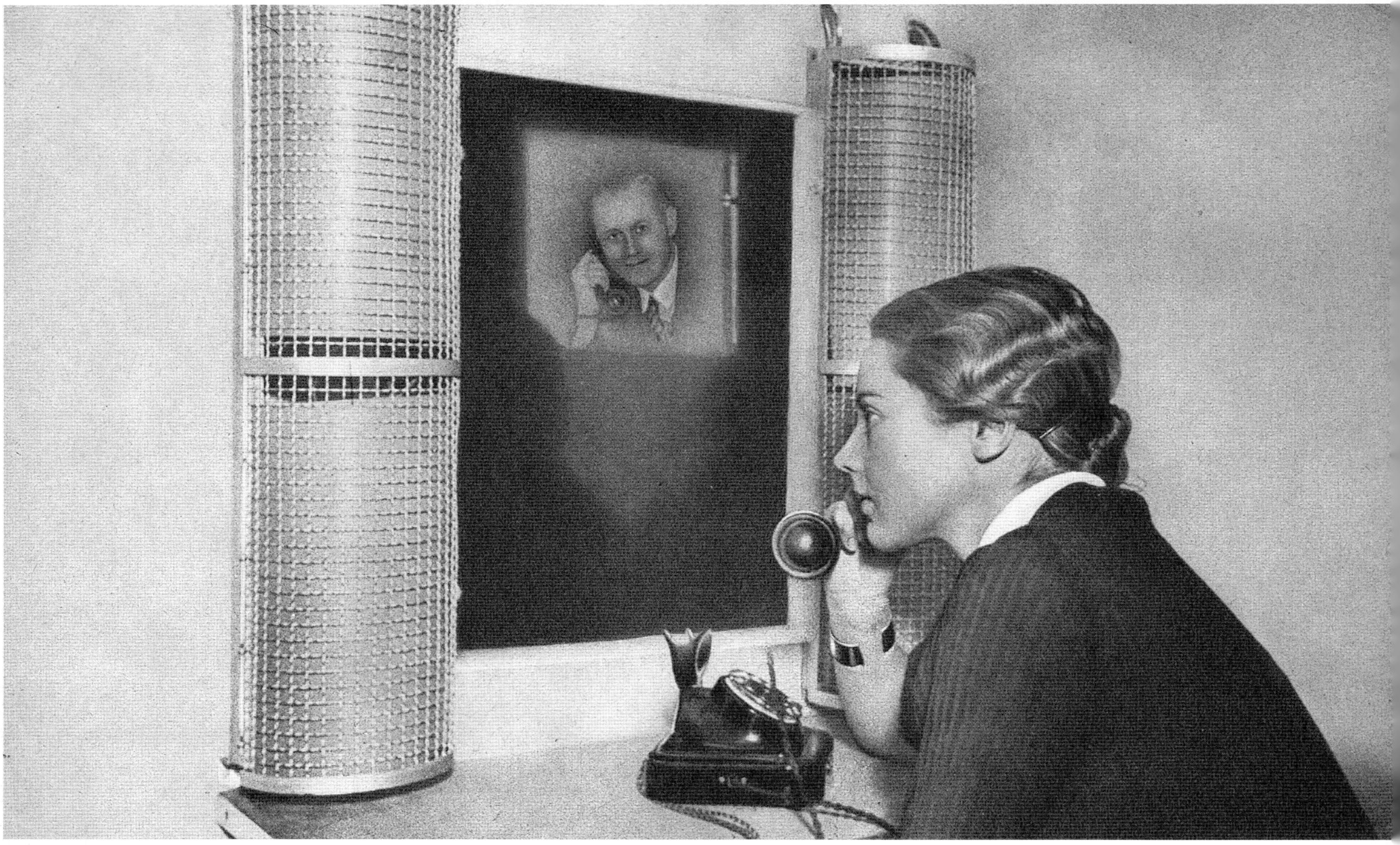

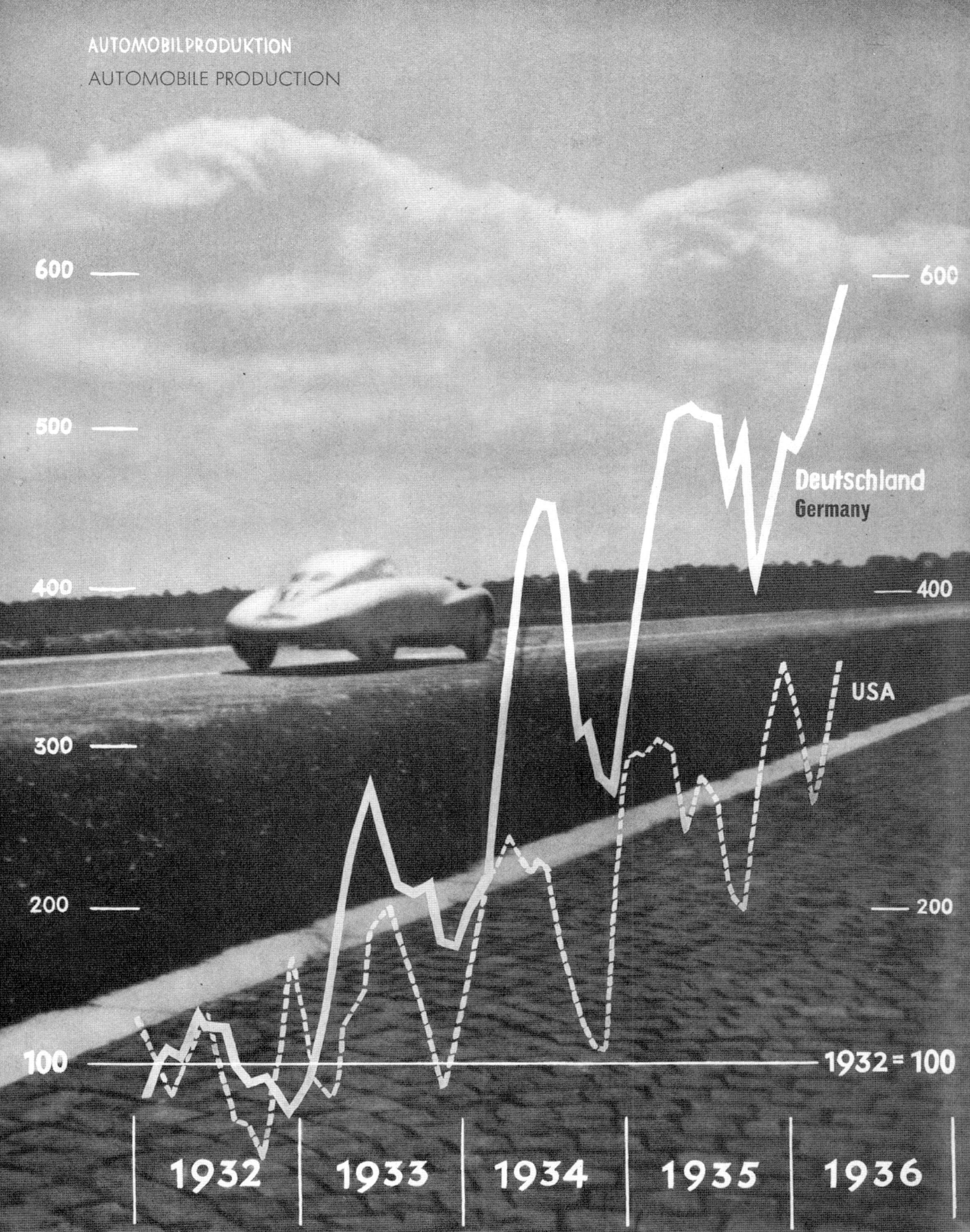

GERMANY WINS THE PRINCIPAL RACES

Germany's automobile development, which up until 1933 was constantly retarded, has made surprising progress since the rise of National Socialism to power. During the first three years of the Third Reich, automobile production increased five-fold. The will of the Führer was behind it.

He also wished to see German cars in the foremost places at the large international races, and this, too, has been accomplished. German racing cars not only succeeded in achieving first places but also second and third, only the Italians being able to interrupt this series of victories now and then.

GERMANY HAS THE FASTEST TRAINS IN THE WORLD

German lightning express trains travel regularly at an average speed of 82 miles per hour. The fastest trains in other countries achieve a top speed of 75 miles.

Below: A new observation car of the German Railway.

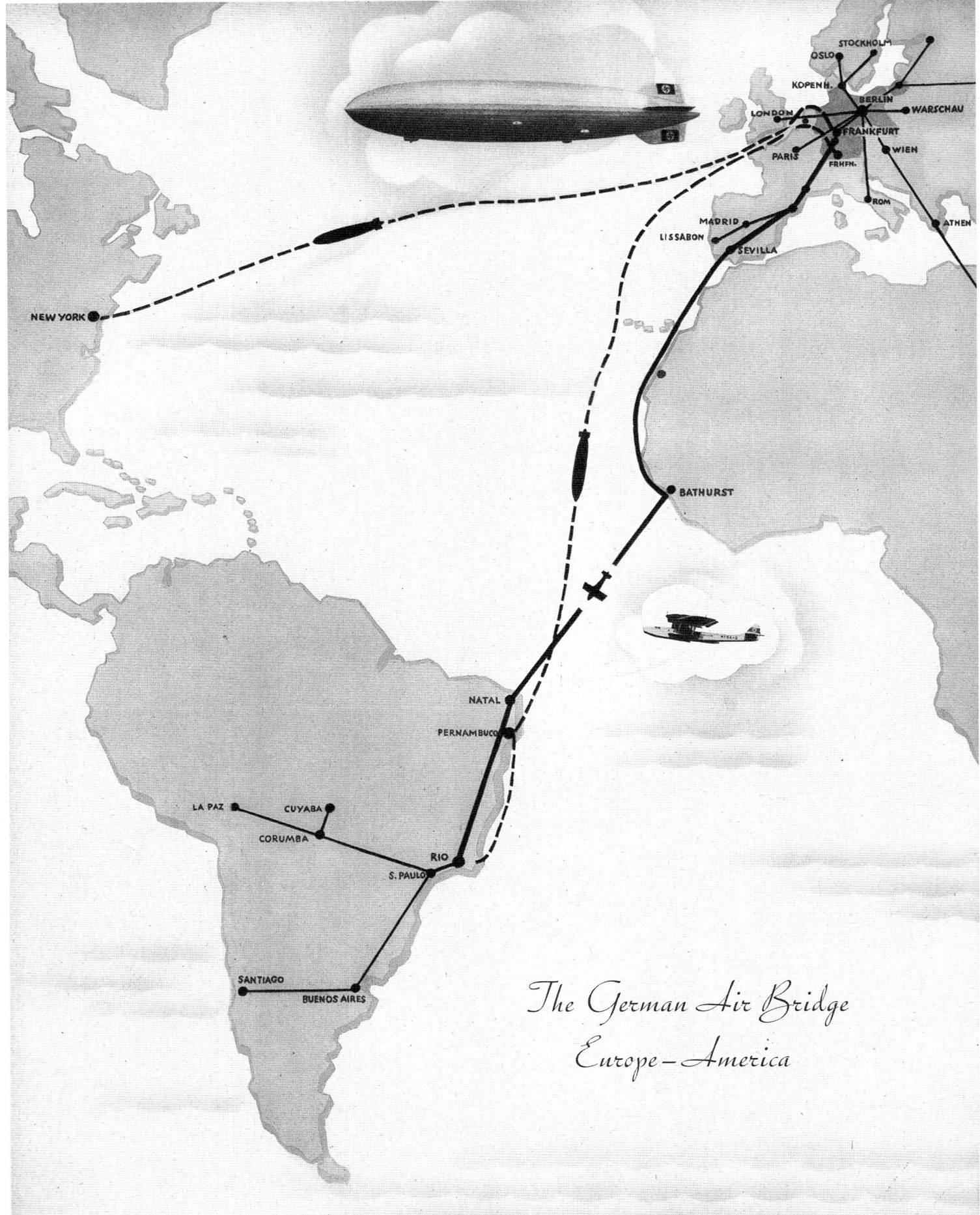

INCOMPARABLE! Like her steamships during an earlier epoch, the German airships are today introducing a new field of travel and communication. The distance between the two hemispheres of the western world has been reduced by half.

Since 1931 the "Graf Zeppelin" has plied regularly between Europe and South America with passengers, mail and freight, requiring only 3½ days for this great distance. Now the gigantic "Hindenburg" is flying between Germany and New York, requiring 2½ days or less than half the time necessary for the steamship voyage.

The 150th ocean crossing by a zeppelin took place in 1936, thousands of passengers have been conveyed, hundreds of tons of mail and freight have been transported, and the total mileage is over one million.

During this entire period not a single accident occurred. Each crossing was made exactly according to schedule and every cabin was booked.

The first airship constructed for transoceanic service, the "Graf Zeppelin", carries 20 passengers, while the "Hindenburg" has accommodations for 50, and a third ship which is now under construction will equal the "Hindenburg" in size.

In her aeroplane service Germany also stands at the top of the world. German mail planes have been flying to South America since 1934, even to the south-western coast and to points far in the interior. The mail is carried to Seville by the fastest transport planes in the world, the "Heinkel", and is there taken on board flying boats for the ocean passage.

Germany possesses the most extensive network of air routes in the world, her international service even including China. Above all, the German air service is the most reliable in existence, since in 1935 only one passenger accident occurred although the total mileage covered was 7½ million.

Hail sacred flame! Hail sacred flag! . . . .

A NATION IN FORM

The German Olympic flame was ignited by the tropical sun of Greece, since it was intended through this symbolic act to propagate the Olympic ideals of Hellenic times in our modern world. These ideals were the highest achievement through perfection of form.

This spirit was present at the Berlin Olympic Festival as never before, especially in the facilities provided for the Games—the magnificent Reich Sport Field, the attractive Olympic Stadium and the efficient, harmonious arrangement of the entire Festival.

But only a nation in form, such as National Socialist Germany, could provide such ideal surroundings. For the first time since antiquity an Olympic Festival was organized which was entirely independent of private interests or facilites. The Führer and the forces of the entire nation stood behind the Berlin Games. The question of financial returns was not even considered, eternal values alone forming the basis for these creations.

The first condition for success in such a project is a definite aim. The manner in which the entire German nation was inspired by this aim was evident when the Olympic Fire arrived at the Stadium, when the Führer appeared each day, or when the victors were honoured. On such occasions every arm was stretched in one direction...

. . . . Hail to the Führer! Hail to the victor!

ATHLETES IN FORM

Olympia was the sanctuary where perfection in human form and achievement was celebrated. The Olympic Stadium in Berlin was also such a sanctuary in gigantic form. It is true that today many are inclined to estimate sporting achievements by the effort rather than perfection of form. Nevertheless, this Festival was a triumph for the ancient ideals. Indescribably attractive performances were achieved, and it was always the most outstanding that led to victory.

In examining the photographs on the succeeding pages which were taken at moments of high Olympic achievement, one can scarcely notice a display of effort but rather a harmonious freedom of every limb, each athlete, however, intent on gaining the victory. In every competition it could be noticed that the victor showed the least effort, while the third and forth competitors seemed to display extreme exertion. This was due to the fact that the latter were struggling with themselves, whereas the former directed all of his efforts towards the one aim—victory.

An entire nation is being trained in sport in the Third Reich. The path to national record achievement is one which requires spiritual and physical perfection of form in the individual. Life will thus be not only stronger and more certain, but also more enjoyable and attractive for all.

Those who display the greatest exertion seldom lead the field. Intent on victory, the winner surges ahead in unrestrained, harmonious form....................

Above: The effortless certainty of the World Champion, Jesse Owens. Below: The World Champion, Helen Stephens, whose running form, however, could be improved.

Which of these 1500 metre runners will be successful? The features of the third athlete, World Champion Lovelock, already reveal a slight smile of victory . . . .

Below: Frl. Krauss, Germany, indicates even at the start of the preliminary races that she knows the path to victory. How uncertain, on the other hand, the last girl to the left!

German Strength!

The German competitors won every throwing competition except one.

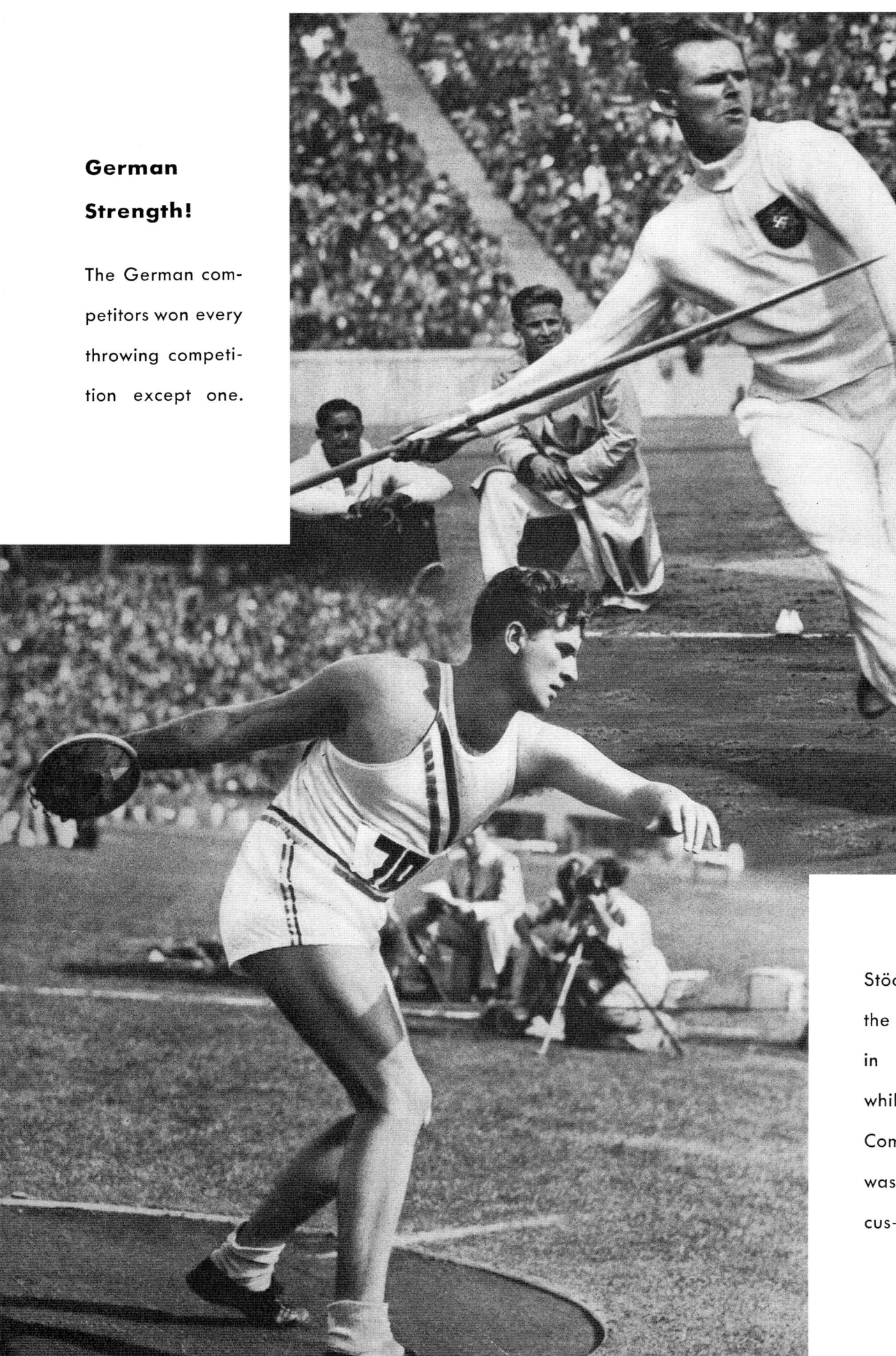

Stöck, Berlin, won the gold medal in javelin-throwing, while Ken Carpenter, Compton, California, was victorious in discus-throwing.

Germany won five gold medals in athletics, all of them in the throwing competitions.

The German hammer-thrower, Hein, exhibits strength and perfection of form. The victory in shot-putting went to Woellke.

German women won two Olympic victories in athletics.

Gisela Mauermayer achieved a "golden" discus-throw, while Tilly Fleischer was victorious in javelin-throwing.

THE JOY OF VICTORY

LAUGHING

VICTORS

OLYMPIC ACHIEVEMENTS

of the New Germany

in 1936

Completion of the first 625 miles of the National Motor Highways, the most gigantic construction project in Europe.

Construction of the Reich Sport Field, the most stupendous sporting centre in the world.

Presentation of the largest and most magnificent of all Olympic Festivals (5,000,000 visitors).

Victory of German sport at the Olympic Games, 33 gold medals being won.

Moreover, five gold medals in the Olympic Art Competition.

Repeated victories of German racing cars in all of the prominent international races.

Max Schmeling's victory over Joe Louis in New York.

Introduction of zeppelin service between Germany and New York.

99 % participation of all authorized voters in an election — a world record.

42,000,000 votes for one candidate (the Führer) — also a world record.

Peaceful recovery of the last remnant of lost sovereign rights (occupation of the Rhineland).

Leaders of Tomorrow

Kommende Führer

HITLER YOUTH! FÜHRER YOUTH!

The creator of the Third Reich has accomplished a mighty construction project.

Still more stupendous, however, will be the results accruing from a development project now taking place within the Reich.

That is the development of the HITLER YOUTH.

The Hitler Youth is the self-governed organization of the young generation of the German people. Following the principle, "Youth must be led by youth", the Führer himself has bestowed unusual rights and powers upon the youth of Germany.

And all that he courageously attempts in the extensive German Reich must also be attempted in its domain by the youth which bears his name. Everything must be started anew.

What was the situation formerly?

On the one side, the oncoming youth was drilled in the lifeless forms of traditional wisdom in the schools, while on the other, it was permitted to go astray in the fields of liberalistic freedom and devote its energies to uncreative groups and causes.

Today, the youth is engaged in mapping out its own existence, and one day will reform the entire sphere of book wisdom.

GERMAN YOUTH TO THE FRONT!

An extremely democratic type of democracy is developing in Germany today, its pattern being the Hitler Youth.

The last effects of the old system of "democratic" government are being experienced in America today. How are the leaders selected there? First, there are the self-appointed professional politicians, this being a name which usually implies "grafter". The respectable political leaders, on the other hand, are largely persons who have succeeded in another profession such as law or business. Most of them are prosperous gentlemen of middle age without any previous political experience who regard the State as a supreme organization for furthering business.

In Germany, the leaders of tomorrow are selected from the youth of today. He who possesses the qualities of leadership becomes a "Führer" among his comrades, and from this time onwards the path of leadership continues unbroken through the Storm Troops and Party directly to the higher political fields of activity without a question of money ever being considered. This is the difference between the two types of leadership. This is National Socialist democracy.

Italian Youth

The Hitler Youth stands alone among the youth organizations of the world in its policy of self-leadership.

The Anglo-Saxon Boy Scouts were originated by and are under the leadership of older persons. The national youth organizations of Italy, Hungary and Russia were created by adults and are under military supervision.

In practically every neighbouring state the youth is armed and its organization is supported by the State. In Russia, rifles are even placed in the hands of the schoolgirls.

Germany alone has no system of military training for her youth. The young men begin their regular period of service at the age of 20.

Soldiers can only be led by experienced adult officers, and the principle of self-leadership in the Hitler Youth forbids this. Nevertheless, it embodies that which is the basis of national strength, namely, the soldierly attitude, implying cooperation, obedience and leadership.

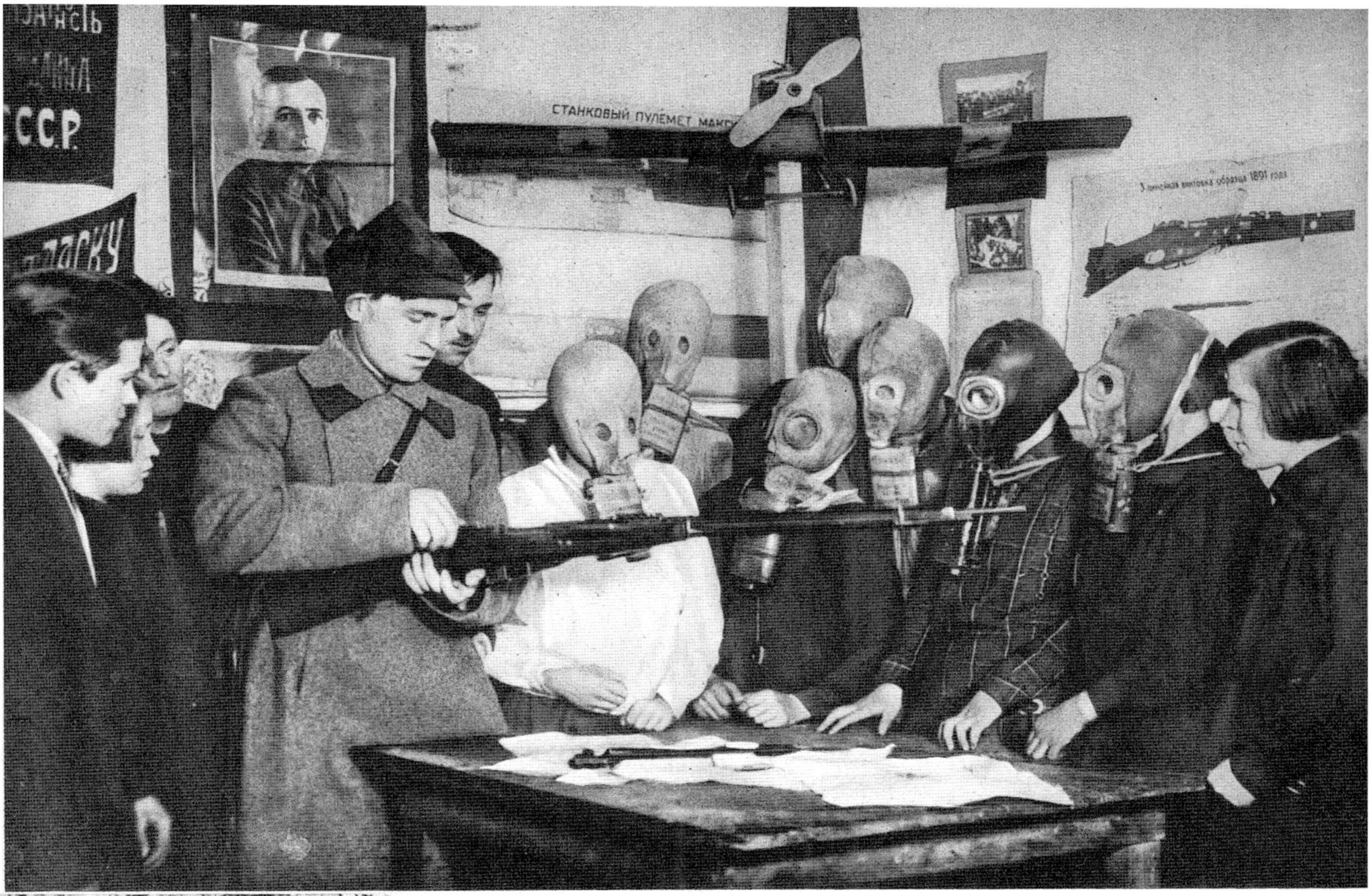

Russian Youth

The neighbouring nations regard Adolf Hitler as a dangerous dictator. The German youth regards him as its ideal, and therefore the name, Hitler Youth. The Führer is the heroic example towards which every youth strives.

This is naturally "dangerous", since it is possible that other nations will become decrepit through their leadership while the German State maintains its progressive, youthful character.

The results of this policy are evident even today. Germany in her impulsive way extends a friendly hand to her neighbours and proposes to remove the roots of dissention through mutual training of the youth on the basis of a common understanding. Instead of responding in the same hearty manner, the other countries cling to their "rights", that is, a traditional "right" to guardianship in Europe. Instead of joyful assent, juridical reproof . . .

This, however, is the attitude of a declining generation. How different would a message from the young heart of France sound!

Voices from Australia

YOUTH SINGS AROUND THE WORLD! 32 NATIONS BROADCAST OVER 700 STATIONS!

The conductor of this cosmic chorus is — the Hitler Youth!

(On October 27th, 1935 the Hitler Youth organized the most gigantic of all radio projects, a broadcast around the world. Youth choruses in every civilized country participated in a programme which was relayed by practically every large radio station in the world.)

"Le Petit Radio", Paris, writes in this connection: "What a magnificent idea to encircle our poor, tortured earth with a band of melodies and songs!... It provides recreation from the international "palaver" and dangerous diplomatic discussions. It is without fear that one realizes that Berlin started this chain of music and devoted all of its well-known ability in technical organization towards perfecting such an idyllic enterprise. From the German youth, which sang the first song, to the Japanese, which ended the programme, it was carried out like a well-ordered orchestral programme. What a wonderful geographic promenade!"

TRUE FRENCH SENTIMENTS!

Voices from South America

GERMANY CALLS THE YOUTH OF THE WORLD!

The Olympic Bell intoned, "I call the youth of the world." The ether waves carry the appeal of young Germany for understanding, and a hearty invitation is sent to every youth: "Visit us and become acquainted."

A special encampment in Germany has been provided for the youth of German descent in every part of the world, and the flag of practically every nation waves over it. From here the young visitors are conveyed throughout the Reich in a 6 mile long motor-coach caravan, the trip covering several weeks. The experiences from these tours are recorded in the Hitler Youth book, "Youth Sees Germany."

There is also the Anglo-German Youth Encampment, and a regular exchange of young visitors takes place between these countries. French and German comrades meet in the student encampments, and the youth organizations from throughout the world are welcome at the many German Youth Hostels with their price of only 30 pfennigs for a night's lodging.

Every Hitler Youth leader is now being sent to foreign countries as a visitor.

The German youth wishes to become acquainted with the world and to further friendly relations between the young generation of every country. Germany calls the youth of the world together!

"AWAY WITH AGE!

Only the eternal young shall be at home in our Germany!

"Youth is an attitude! The crippled Chamberlain exemplified eternal youth just as did Goethe until his last days. "Faust", the "Ninth Symphony" and the will of Adolf Hitler are eternally young, recognizing neither age nor transition. There are men, however, who pass their lives as greybeards; their chill paralyses every timid movement of a new life. Only the united forces of a courageous youth is able to destroy them!"

The Reich Youth Leader

The Reich Youth Leader BALDUR von SCHIRACH is descended on his mother's side from American pioneers who played a prominent role in the founding of the United States. He thus combines in his person the noblest American and German heritages. In its leader as well as its principles the German youth bridges all frontiers and oceans.

IN A SCHOOL FOR HITLER YOUTH WOMEN LEADERS

IRRESISTIBLE

YOUTH

GERMAN YOUTH . . . .

.... HITLER YOUTH

A SINGLE COMRADESHIP!

The Hitler Youth Organization comprises 6,000,000 German boys and girls. Ninety per cent of all those between 10 and 14 years of age are already members, and before long the total will have reached 100 per cent. Those who emerge from this period of training will be taken into the Party. This is the pathway to State leadership, and it is open to every young German.

COMRADESHIP IN PRACTICE!

In the weekly gatherings the youth learns what it means to be German, realizes that class distinctions do not exist and that all are bound to the Fatherland by the same fate. Saturday, however, is the day of youth, and the young nation meets at encampments in the woods and hills, for sport and games, and for comradeship in sunshine or storm on native soil.

Active in Sport . . . .

.... Carefree in Recreation

LONG HIKES EVERY SUMMER . . . .

.... AND SEVERAL WEEKS OF CAMP LIFE

FUTURE LEADERS

acquire technical training. An entire department of the Hitler Youth is devoted to seamanship. It leads the world in the field of gliding. It possesses a Reich Radio School for training a corps of radio technicians, and has its own programme director at every German broadcasting station.

RADIO EXPERTS

The Hitler Youth plays a leading role in German broadcasting, and in its round the world broadcast with over 700 stations participating it even assumed the leadership. Practically every day its broadcasts are sent to all parts of the world by means of Germany's powerful short-wave station, and are regular features on the German programme.

AVIATION ....

.... SPORT OF THE GERMAN YOUTH

OLYMPIAD OF WORK

THE REICH PROFESSION COMPETITION: 1,800,000 CONTESTANTS!

This most extensive test of ability and most stupendous competition in the world is organized each year by the Hitler Youth.

"Diligent youth stood at the work-bench or lathe, paved a section of roadway, ploughed or designed — the overwhelming creative urge of the youth found a new means of expression. It was not a question of money or gain but of the accomplishment itself and the honour which was accorded the victor in a professional group for his achievement. The working youth realized with joy that his work and he himself were unconditionally recognized and honoured, and that the attention of the entire German nation was concentrated upon his profession competition."
Baldur von Schirach

Town and Country — HAND in HAND

AWAY FROM THE CITY STREETS ....

One can only say: "Such an institution should be universal." Naturally!
Nevertheless, the new Germany alone possesses
THE LAND YEAR
Each Easter girls and boys who have sat at the school benches for eight years and who have spent fourteen years confined by metropolitan life begin their "Land Year". Away from the city tenements and back courts to the encampments and the peasants! Here, at the source of all life, these children of the exhausted cities acquire new vigour before they are again swallowed up by the offices and factories.

The Land Year is accredited as the ninth school year, and those who are summoned by it are obliged to go. Life during the Land Year is described as follows by the director of an encampment:

"During the first weeks he became a peasant — but did so gladly. That was the change. Paved streets and tenements ceased to exist under the free heavens, and the statement of the Führer concerning the nobility of work achieved a deeper significance. Eight months — from the first green of the young shoots to the December frost — provided a wealth of personal experience, establishing a contact with the true religion of nature."

.... TO OPEN NATURE!

Excerpt from a letter:

"We were Berlin girls, quite proud of the fact that we came from the metropolis and were not land 'yokels'.

"As I entered the garden for the first time and was told to dig, my attitude changed. The spade was too heavy, the soil too hard, the sun too hot and my muscles too weak. Finally, I gave it up, but during the noonday rest period I thought to myself: If I were only a land 'yokel' and strong enough for such work, wouldn't it be wonderful? But nonsense! Naturally, I as a city girl could do it too—if only the sun were not so hot—and the spade not so heavy—and the soil not so hard...

"We changed gradually. We noticed every day how hard the peasant works, and realized that he is not stupid but very clever. He is an expert in his way. What would we city children do without the peasant? And the word, 'yokel', was no longer heard in our encampment..."

Irmgard Prell, Ringitten Land Year, East Prussia.

THE LAND YEAR HOMES accommodate at the present time 32,500 city children, and it is intended that one day the young city populace of the entire nation shall have the advantage of this form of schooling. Housekeeping, weaving, economy, agriculture and natural geography are learned here, although experience counts far more than mere knowledge. Instead of teachers, there are leaders, and instead of drubbing, living.

A cool plunge is also included!

ON THE FARM there is work to be done. It is here that the peasant shares his fundamental knowledge with his young metropolitan assistants. In this manner, a bond of mutual respect is drawn between the city and the farm. A touch of the city is brought to the country, and the atmosphere of the harvest is carried into the town.

Peasant children from the metropolis!

HOW MANY NATIONS IN THE HISTORY OF THE WORLD HAVE DETERIORATED BECAUSE LIFE WAS CONCENTRATED IN THE CITIES?

THE GERMAN NATION, HOWEVER, SHALL REMAIN ETERNALLY YOUNG!

"For eight months on end no single day resembled another, so that a schedule can only indicate all that happened. Reveille—morning run—making beds—hoisting the flag—singing—breakfast—labour service in the village—lunch—sport and games—schooling—supper—rest... With outside and inside work, exertion and relaxation each day dawned and died.

"Games in the open—hikes and camp life—night marches and camp fires with songs—music, readings and stories—national celebrations—village festivals—these and a hundred other experiences constitute a reserve of vitality which evidences itself in the accomplishments and attitude of the future men and women...

"The long hike provided the climax of the Land Year—the marching column with the flags and drummers at the head. No one could miss this occasion. Each had to assert himself in whichever capacity he was placed.

"Land and people, woods, streams, lakes and mountains created a new feeling of life—the proud sensation of being a definite part of it."

Land Year Home Leader Fritzsche (in "International Educational Magazine")

HAPPY RECRUITS FOR THE LABOUR SERVICE

Compulsory Labour Service of various kinds has been common for centuries. The Pharaohs based their almost divine power upon forced labour, and all of the peasants during the Middle Ages were obliged to work for their feudal lord.

This type of exploitation of the nation's man power has been customary with every dictator, but it took the genius of a Führer to elevate this work to the plain of honorary service.

The German Führer not only succeeded in doing this, but has changed the old compulsory service into one of willing cooperation.

A whole generation of German youths is at work on the mountains and moors and is deriving untold pleasure from its work. These youths are enthusiastic in relating their experiences, and are even proud of their common achievement with the spade.

How is this possible? Principally because the spirit of leadership has penetrated to the most obscure group leader, and all those who inspire enthusiasm in their colleagues are leaders.

This is Adolf Hitler's CONQUERING ARMY!

It is engaged in conquering sections larger than Alsace-Lorraine or the Polish Corridor. Its weapon is invincible, its victory certain.

THE HIGH SCHOOL OF THE NATION

200,000 German youths are passing through this school of work. It is here that the "aristocratic" students meet the sons of workers from the mines and tenements. Everything is equalized on the common basis of peaceful cooperation for the people and the Reich. An incomparable process of democratizing!

The Labour Service Law contains the following statements:

1. The Reich Labour Service is a service of honour to the German people.
2. Every young German of either sex is obliged to serve his country in the Reich Labour Service.
3. Through the Labour Service the German youth will be trained in the spirit of National Socialism and mutual cooperation so that it will acquire a healthy attitude towards work and respect for craftmanship.
4. The Reich Labour Service is organized for the execution of tasks which will benefit the entire nation.

In this connection the Führer declared: "It is a stupendous undertaking to educate an entire nation to this new conception of work. We have nevertheless begun, and shall succeed."

THIS LAND WILL SOON BE COVERED WITH RIPENING GRAIN!

New land is wrested from the sea, and the fertility of farming land increased; waste land is planted with trees, dry land irrigated and swamps drained by the Labour Service members.

A DAY IN THE LABOUR SERVICE

- 6.00: Reveille — Early Morning Exercises
- 7.00: Breakfast — Parade
- 7.30: Off to Work
- 10.00: Refreshment Pause
- 2.30: Return to Camp
- 3.00: Lunch
- 4.00: Physical Training
- 5.00: Instruction
- 6.00: General Assembly — Issuing of Orders
- 7.15: Evening Meal
- 7.45: Time for Cleaning and Repairing
- 8.15: Evening Entertainment
- 10.00: Lights Out.

IN OTHER WORDS:

6 hours of field work
1½ hours of gymnastics and sport
1 hour of instruction
2 hours of general assembly for conversation, singing, reading, games and entertainment
Camp leave on Sundays and twice during the week

THE GUIDING PRINCIPLES

1. Learning to work
2. Training in national cooperation
3. Economic independence

Service age: 19 years

Service period: 6 months at the present time.

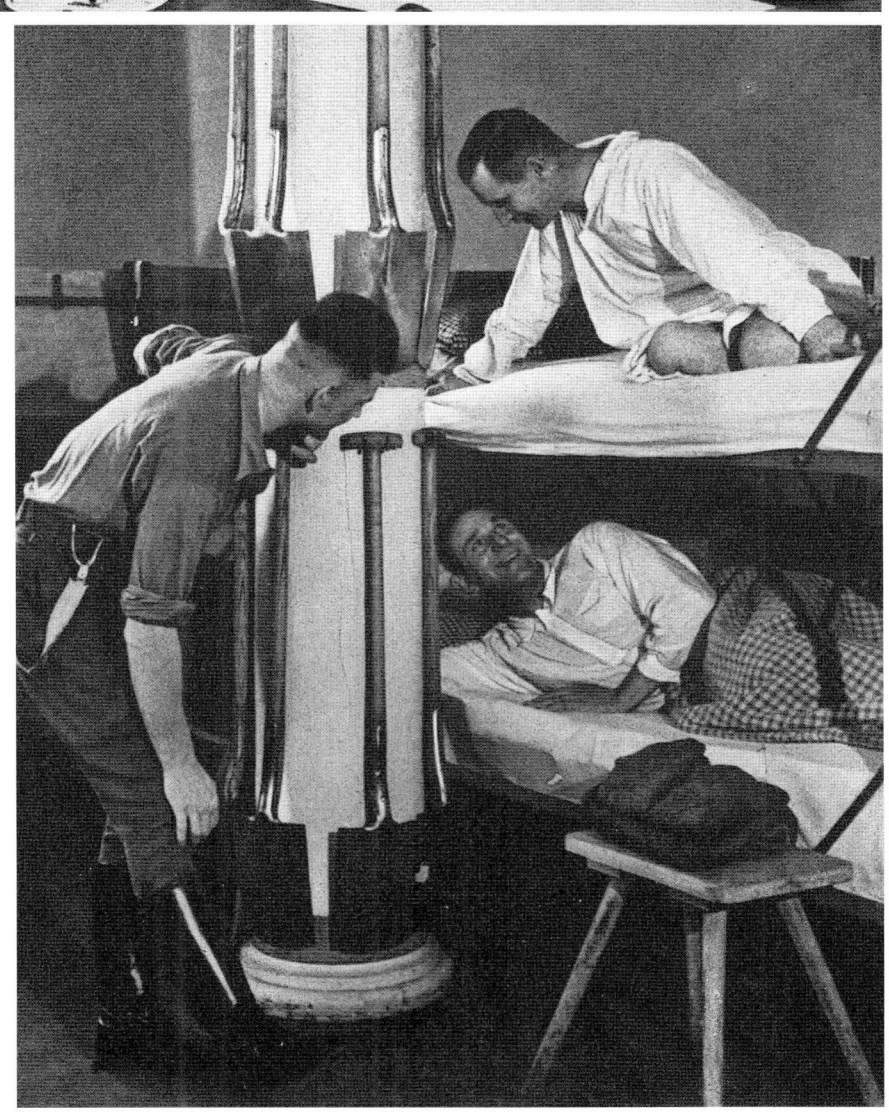

REICH LABOUR SERVICE LEADER HIERL GIVES ORDERS . . . .

AND THE CONQUEST OF THE LAND BEGINS!

7 1/2 million acres of moor and swamp land are to be reclaimed and made arable.

12 1/2 million acres are to be irrigated.

20 million acres are to be rendered productive through proper drainage.

Even during the winter, young Germany is cheerfully at work undeterred by the weather.

The Labour Service prepares the land, including the planting of trees and laying out of streets then come the builders.

............AND A NEW LIFE BECOMES ROOTED IN THE GERMAN SOIL

For the settler this means his own existence, and to the German people, their daily bread. Formerly, millions were spent in foreign countries in order to feed the German nation, but within a short time this situation will be remedied to a large extent. Germany will never again face the menace of starvation thanks to the efforts of the Labour Service.

THE WOMEN'S.

According to the Reich Labour Service Law, every young German is obliged to perform this honorary service for the welfare of the nation.

The Women's Service, however, must be feminine in nature. There must be no barrack life or Amazon columns for the future mothers of Germany, but proper homes and individual tasks. Years of preparation are required in order to arrange this life in the proper manner, and for the time being the Women's Labour Service includes only 12,000 volunteers.

Their homes are small and usually situated in villages, settlements or distressed areas, although they are also to be found in industrial centres. Wherever it is most necessary, the Women's Labour Service is on hand.

Less assuming, but at the same time filled with more responsibility and demanding greater sacrifice than the men's service is that of the women — just like their task in life.

...LABOUR SERVICE

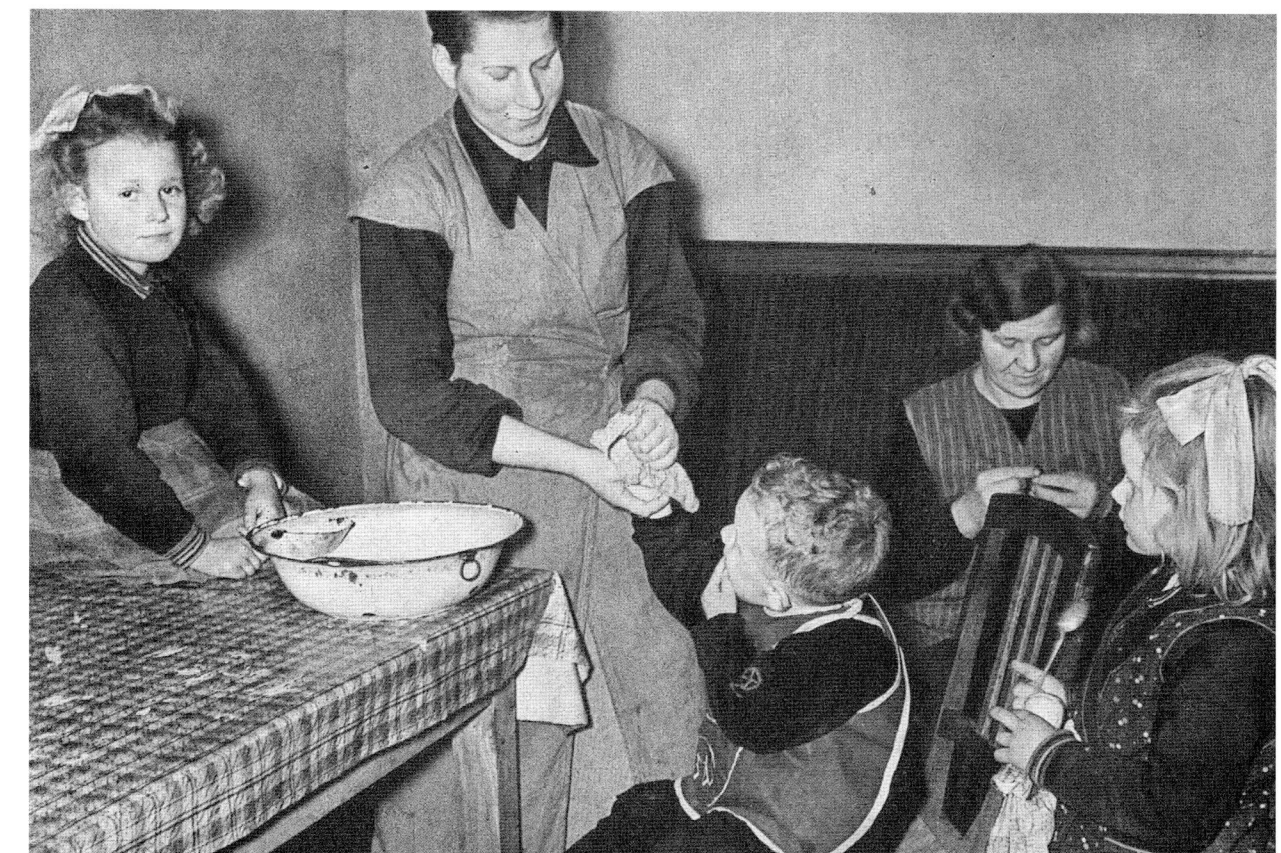

THEY WRITE:

"If you could only see me here, you would certainly be astonished. I work in a peasent family until eight o'clock in the evening and I was extremely proud when the wife requested our leader to send me. Can you understand this — that one does all the daily chores for the sick wife of a peasant and is proud of it? When you are able to understand, you will comprehend the true significance of the Labour Service."

"Four weeks ago I was still sitting over my books, but now I work with a spade, sleep on straw and do the chores of a stable boy. When I occupied myself with reading, I was unhappy; now, however, I delve into the earth instead of books. I do not wish to accept a ready-made philosophy of life in the manner of a new coat, but rather to find my own way. I could not discover this in books, allthough now I feel that I am really living."

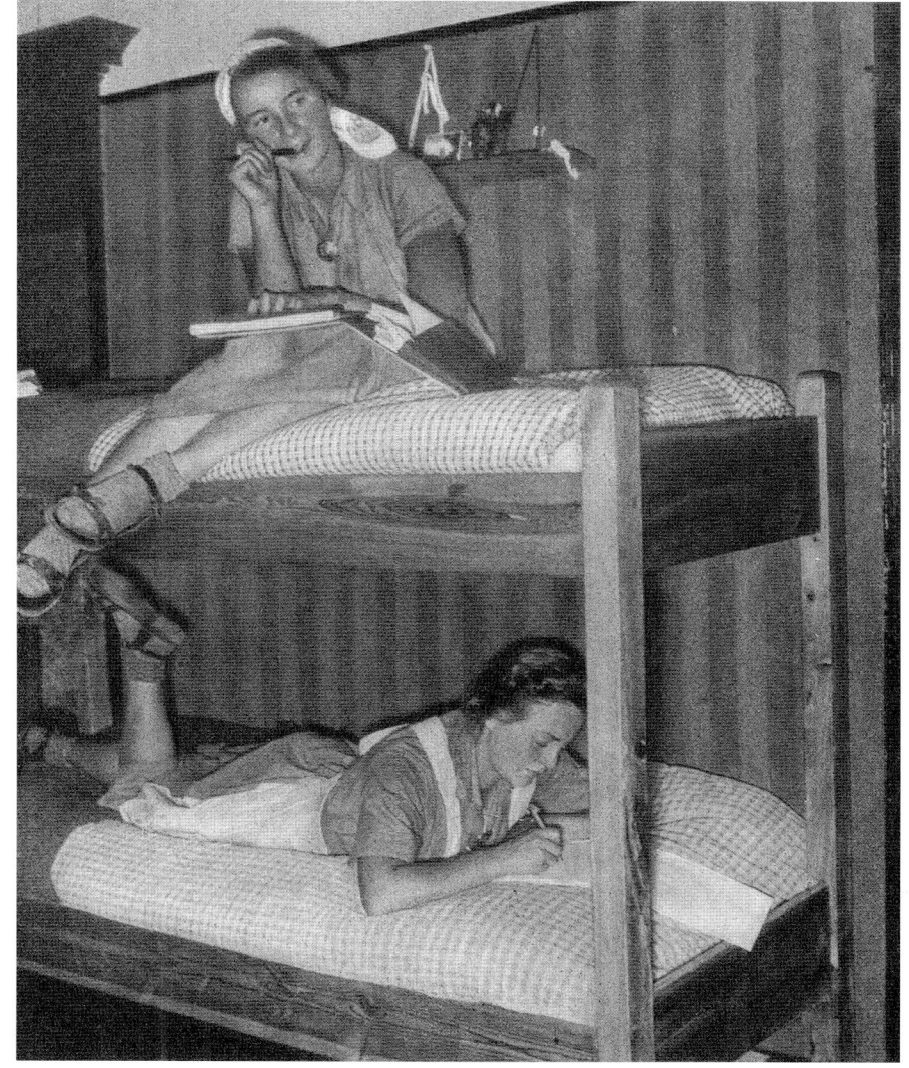

A high school graduate at the college of work.

$12\,{}^1/_2\,{}^0/_0$ of the Labour Service girls are students.

(From now on, no one will be admitted to the university who has not completed her Labour Service.)

This cowgirl is a peasant's daughter, but her companions are from the study hall and accounting department.

Venerable looms are found in many Labour Service homes, and the young generation is eager to try its hand.

(A school for teaching hand-weaving has been founded in the new Reich.)

Rural life is extremely interesting to these amateurs, but they also become acquainted with its more serious aspects.

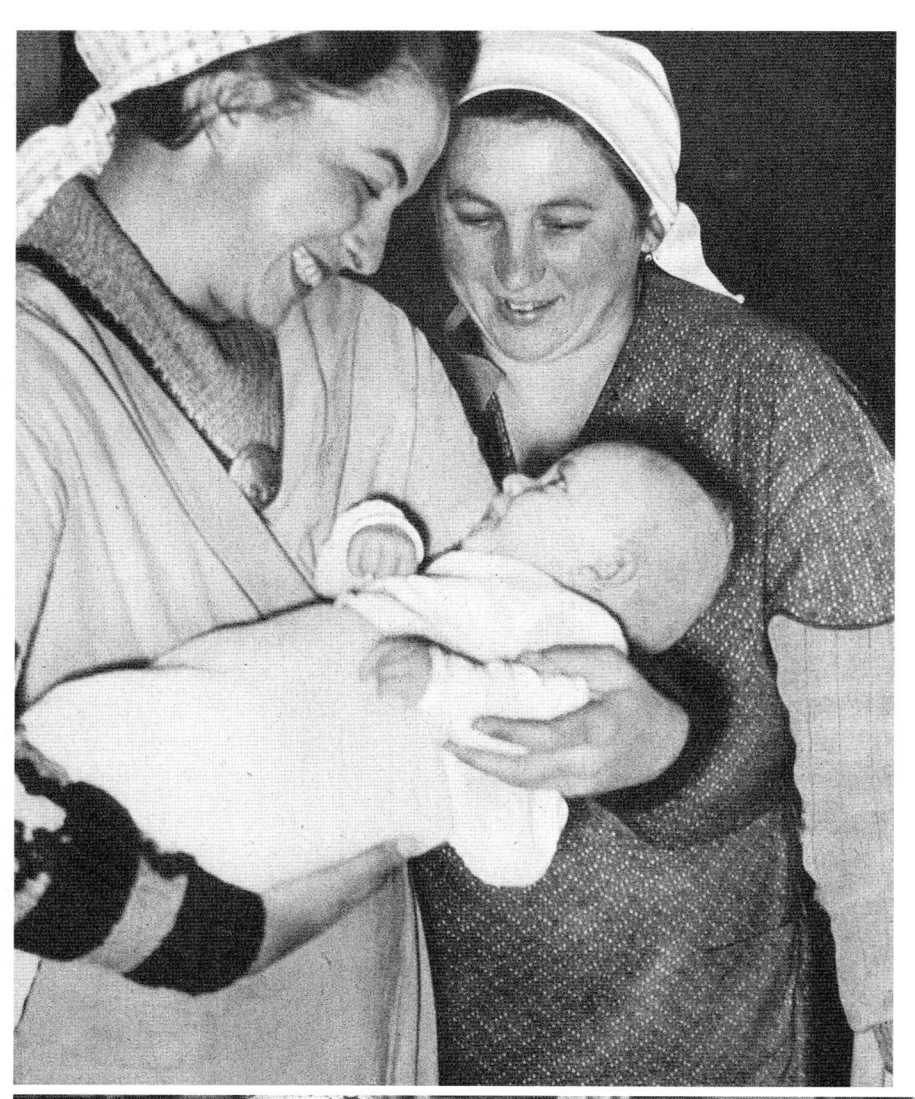

The principal task of the Women's Labour Service is assisting overworked wives and mothers.

Wherever distress is present, the Labour Service girls are ready to help.

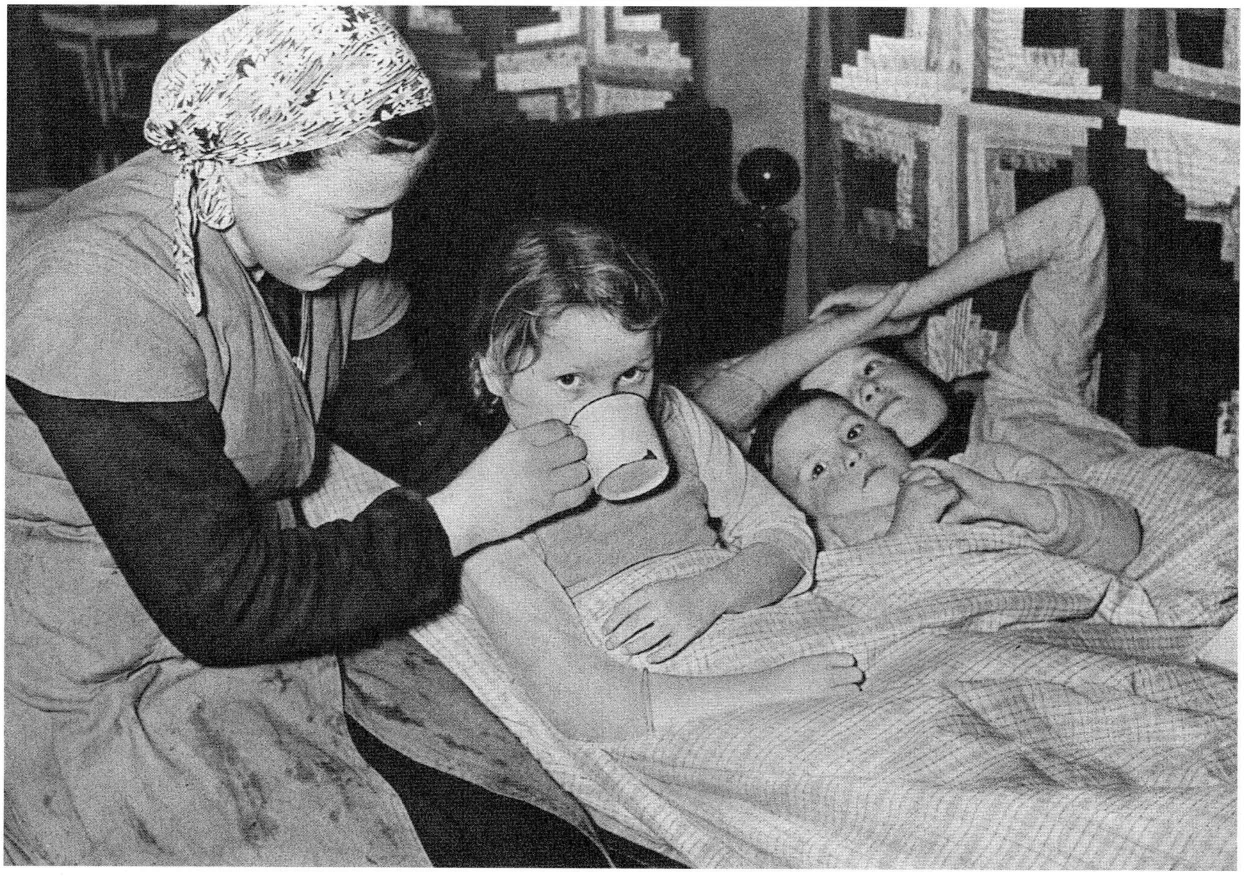

The daughter of influential parents performing her Labour Service in Emsland writes as follows: "Here among our settlers where there is more work to be done than people to do it, each of us has her task. The refuse which we do not remove remains to become a menace to health, the clothes which we do not mend become more and more shabby, and what we do not teach the children they do not learn. The worry which we are not able to alleviate continues. I am especially happy to be able to do my bit."

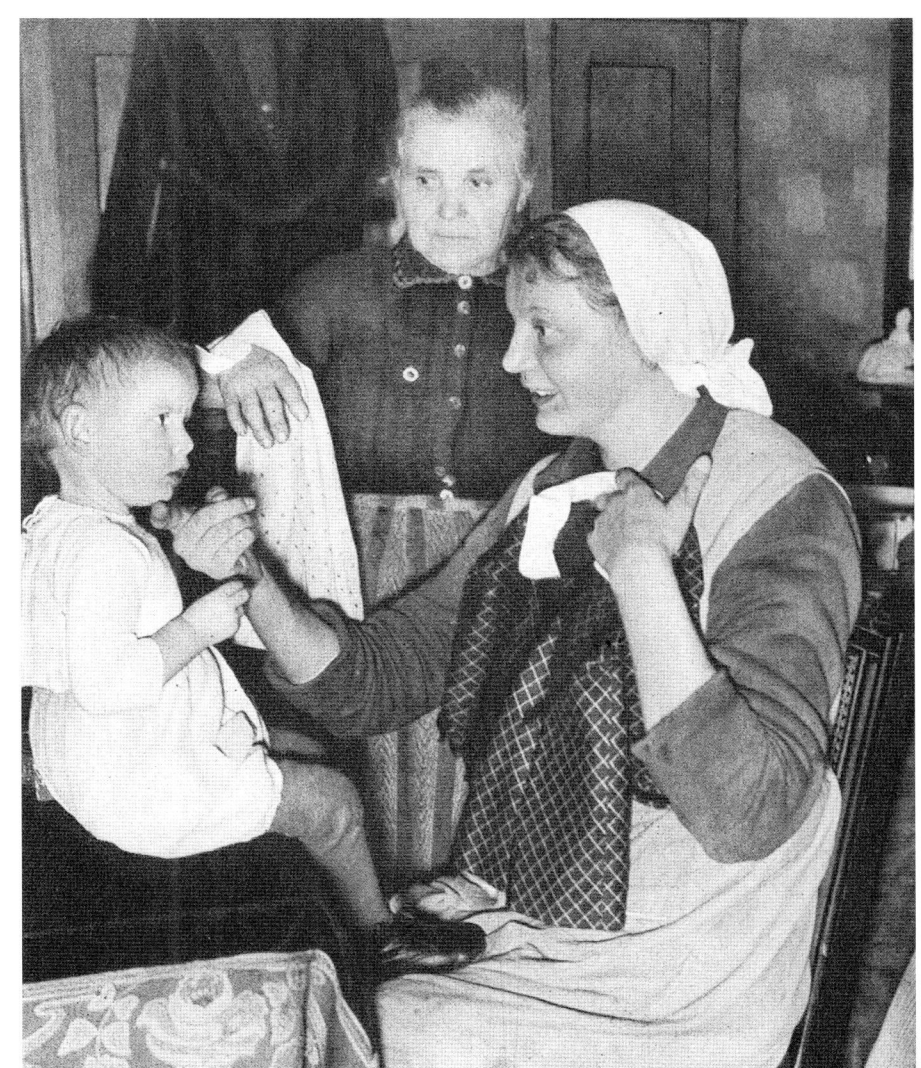

Peasant:	What do you wish, You, who come from the city?
City Girls:	We heard the cry of distress in our homeland. We wish to help — rescue — create, To reap the golden grain, To assist you as we can, for you provide the bread, You rescue the Fatherland from starvation!
Peasant:	You are too weak; You cannot endure! You are lacking in strength; your hands are soft!
City Girls:	We shall accomplish it! You must trust us, Must have confidence in our work. We have the will, and that gives us courage — The will to sustain our farms and homes! Depend on us and accept our aid!
Both:	We shall strive together for the Fatherland.

COMMUNITY SPIRIT — — *The SA Santa Claus*

VOLKS GEMEINSCHAFT

Der SA-Weihnachtsmann

COMRADESHIP IN THE RANKS

In spite of all the misfortune of the World War, it had one beneficial effect: It fostered the feeling of comradeship at the front and at home. America also experienced this, and wished to preserve the spirit of unity for all time. But the time was not ripe in America, and it was only in Germany that fertile ground was present, a ground made rich through suffering and distress.

COMRADE-SHIP IN LIFE AND DEATH

One who sponsored the cause of German unity from the very beginning was the front line soldier, Adolf Hitler, and it is due to this spirit of comradeship which grew out of the War that he ascended to power. His entire policy is soldierly in character, and no nation whose conscience is clear need have fear. War-like agitation against neighbouring nations is forbidden in the New Reich. These ranks of German men signify something quite different.

NATIONAL SOCIALIST COMRADES WITH SMALL GUESTS

NATIONAL SOCIALISM? What does it mean? The true significance of this name given to the German movement is usually overlooked, and the hasty reader at the breakfast table is prone to see—"National...ism".

THE GERMAN FLAG? What does it look like? The majority of foreigners know that it contains a swastika and believe that this signifies only—"National...ism".

THE FLAG BEARERS? Who are they? The world regards their disciplined ranks, the brown uniforms and reflects—"National...ism".

It is time, however, to wake up! S O C I A L I S M is the principle world in the title of the Movement. The basic colour in its banner is R E D and those who wear the brown uniforms are C O M R A D E S!

PREMIER AND CARPENTER

National Socialism is German Socialism,

which signifies

NATIONAL COMRADESHIP

COMRADE GOEBBELS COLLECTS FOR NEEDY MEMBERS OF THE NATIONAL COMMUNITY

The complete title of the Führer's Party is NATIONAL SOCIALIST GERMAN WORKERS' PARTY. In other words, not merely a National and German, but a SOCIALIST WORKERS' PARTY was led to power by the Führer—a fact which is overlooked by the majority of foreigners—and by many Germans as well. This failure to read correctly has led to many false conceptions of the Movement.

Separate emphasis on the two component parts of the Party is also false since "National German Party" would signify bourgeois class domination, while "Socialist Workers' Party" would imply rule by the proletariat.

It is this idea of class distinction that the Führer wishes to abolish, but the old capitalistic ideology, which has always tended to look down upon work and the worker, stands in the way, and therefore the National Socialist German Workers' Party is carrying out a thorough process of house-cleaning.

WORKER HITLER AMONG HIS TOILING COMRADES

National Comradeship

is

WORKERS' COMRADESHIP

Factory superintendents and workers together at a training school of the Labour Front

NATIONALISM — NATIONAL COMRADESHIP — WORKERS' COMRADESHIP

The Führers' Deputy, Reich Minister Hess, among working comrades

The Reich Organizing Leader, Dr. Ley, among fellow workers

The world-famous Gewandhaus Orchestra of Leipzig plays a symphony concert in the midst of the machines and lathes of a large manufacturing plant for the benefit of working comrades.

Employers spend millions in order to improve the working surroundings.

A chorus of workers performs in the dramatic presentation, "Honour and Work": "Thus we are called; nameless our ranks — but 'tis we who pave the way to eternity. Nation work on!"

A social gathering of the workers in the club rooms installed by a factory.

COMRADES TOGETHER

Women students substitute for workers in factories and mills so that the latter may enjoy a vacation. The wages earned by the temporary workers are paid to the permanent employees.

National Socialism —
German Socialism —
NATIONAL COMRADESHIP

A TRUE STORY
(with authentic photographs)

Fräulein Herta of the wine department always had a friendly smile for customers.

She herself, however, had seen little of the sunny side of life.

Then one day Fräulein Herta was informed that she was to have a 14 day vacation and would make a long sea journey to the sunny South.

Fräulein Herta received this wonderful news with tears of joy.

IN THE SUNNY SOUTHLAND

Herta, the sales girl

is now served by others

OFF TO MADEIRA!

The generous benefactor who enabled Fräulein Herta to make a sea journey was the well-known Berlin department store where she was employed. And the benevolent spirit which inspired this firm is called "Strength through Joy".

Thousands of workers are enabled through similar sea voyages to refresh their strength through joyful recreation, this being financed partly by themselves and partly by the firm for which they work. The costs of such vacations are kept so low, however, that every thrifty citizen is able to participate.

The "Strength through Joy" fleet, which will soon number 8 and eventually 32 ships, will convey the German workers to the North and South in summer and winter.

Most of the "Strength through Joy" vacationists, however, prefer to visit their own native country, and today are able to travel to every part of the Reich where they are joyfully welcomed by their countrymen—not as strangers but as friends.

Hundreds of thousands from the factories and mills take long hiking trips, and even the traditional "Wander Year" of the apprentices has been reintroduced through the exchange of jobs. The Germans abroad are also to be given an opportunity of becoming acquainted with their Fatherland through "Strength through Joy" voyages.

EVERY CITIZEN WILL ENJOY A VACATION TRIP

A fantastic plan! But all of the accomplishments of the Third Reich were once regarded as "fantastic plans".

The Labour Front is making rapid progress in this direction with its 5,000,000 annual vacationists, many of whom had never before been able even to consider such a luxury. All of the available vacation sites are thus taken.

What next? Create new vacation possibilities—in fact, enough for three times as many people as at present. A new "Strength through Joy" sea resort is being constructed at Rügen where a half million workers will enjoy a vacation each summer. New "Strength through Joy" ships are being built, all with outside cabins and wide, spacious decks—floating recreation homes for Germany's workers. Throughout the country large vacation homes are being erected in the most attractive locations.

The use of all these facilities may be enjoyed for the small sum of about 2 marks per day, this including travel and meals.

Finally, every worker is to be provided with a free two-week vacation trip which, according to law, will be paid for in the form of auxiliary wages. The youth has already been considered through the institution of Hitler Youth encampments, but the New Reich does not intend to leave the mothers, the small children and the old people at home.

A VISIT TO THE NORTHERN FJORDS WITH "STRENGTH THROUGH JOY"

("Strength through Joy" is the department of the German Labour Front which interests itself exclusively in the recreation of the workers. The Labour Front is a common organization which includes all of the German workers, both employers and employees.)

Two such 25,000 ton "Strength through Joy" vacation ships will soon be completed.

IN THE PEOPLE'S THEATRE

SUNRISE IN GERMANY

A ticket costs 50 pfennigs, and every seat in the People's Theatre is one price. It is decided by lot who will sit in a loge and who in the gallery.

Cheap, is it not? But what does it mean in the life of the people? It means that millions who formerly sat at home evening after evening now have the opportunity of enjoying theatrical entertainment.

That millions were formerly unable to enjoy such pleasures is conclusively proved in the results of a questionnaire circulated throughout the extensive Siemens Firm in Berlin a few years ago. From the answers submitted by everyone from director down to messenger boy it was revealed that 70% of these workers had never been inside a theatre. This 70% is now included in the German Labour Front, and in Berlin alone seven "Strength through Joy" theatres are constantly sold out. This means that a million and a half workers visit the theatre each year.

Arrangements are also made for the workers to visit the museums, and in cases where the factories are located at considerable distances, the museums are brought to the workers, hundreds of such exhibitions having already been organized. The activities of the "Strength through Joy" department in the factories and villages are also extensive, including concerts, lectures, festive evenings, etc. The total number of participants in these undertakings throughout the Reich is already 25,000,000.

Isolated villages and distressed areas are provided with free entertainment by the "Strength through Joy" travelling cinema.

They had never seen anything like this before. But the traveling cinema will come again before long............

THE THEATRE............

. COMES TO THE PEOPLE!

Cocoa and rolls: The S. S. official with the travelling cinema brings something for hungry stomachs as well as entertainment for the eyes and ears . . . . . .

"Strength through Joy" travelling theatres are also to be found throughout the Reich. A performance is being given here for the workers on the National Motor Highway.

"STRENGTH THROUGH JOY"

SUMMONS ALL

TO

SPORT!

3,000,000 comrades are already participating!

THE SPORT

OF THE MILLIONAIRE

HAS BECOME

THE SPORT OF THE PEOPLE!

German workers
enjoy
yachting!

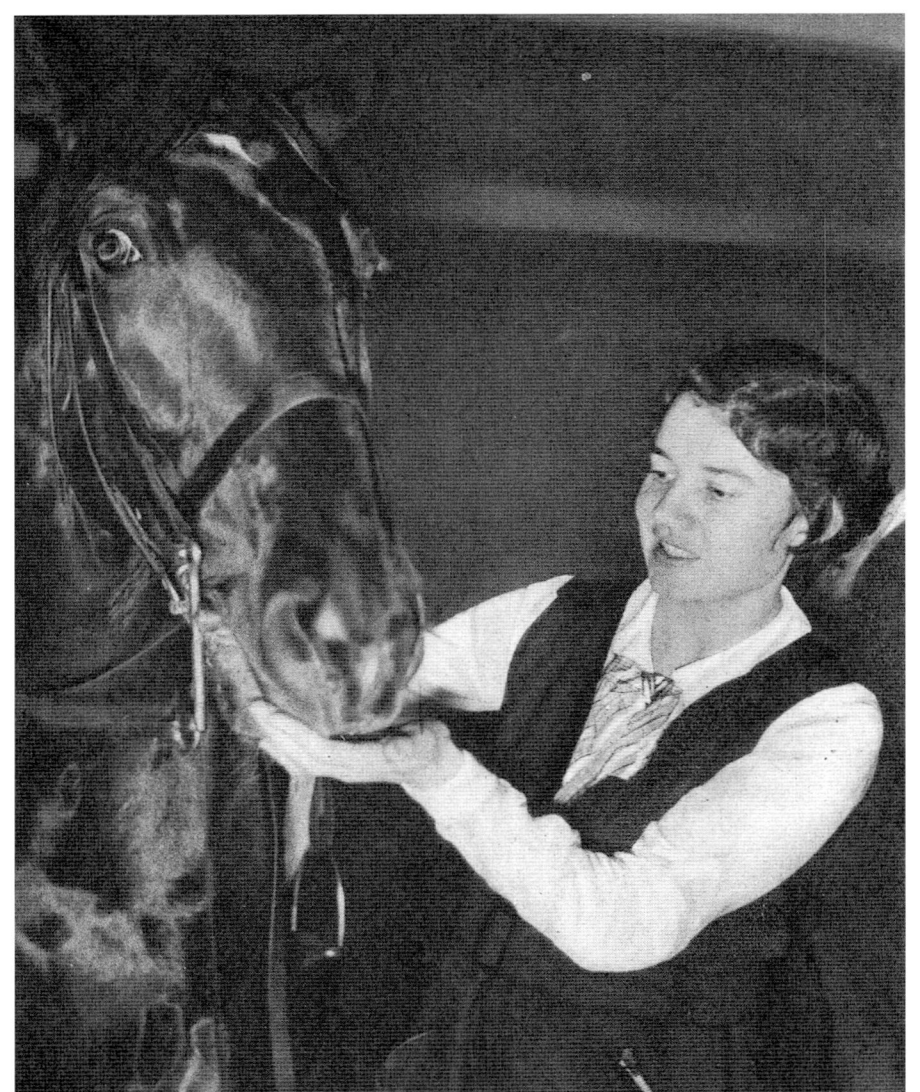

LIKE A BANKER'S DAUGHTER

In a "Strength through Joy" skiing cabin

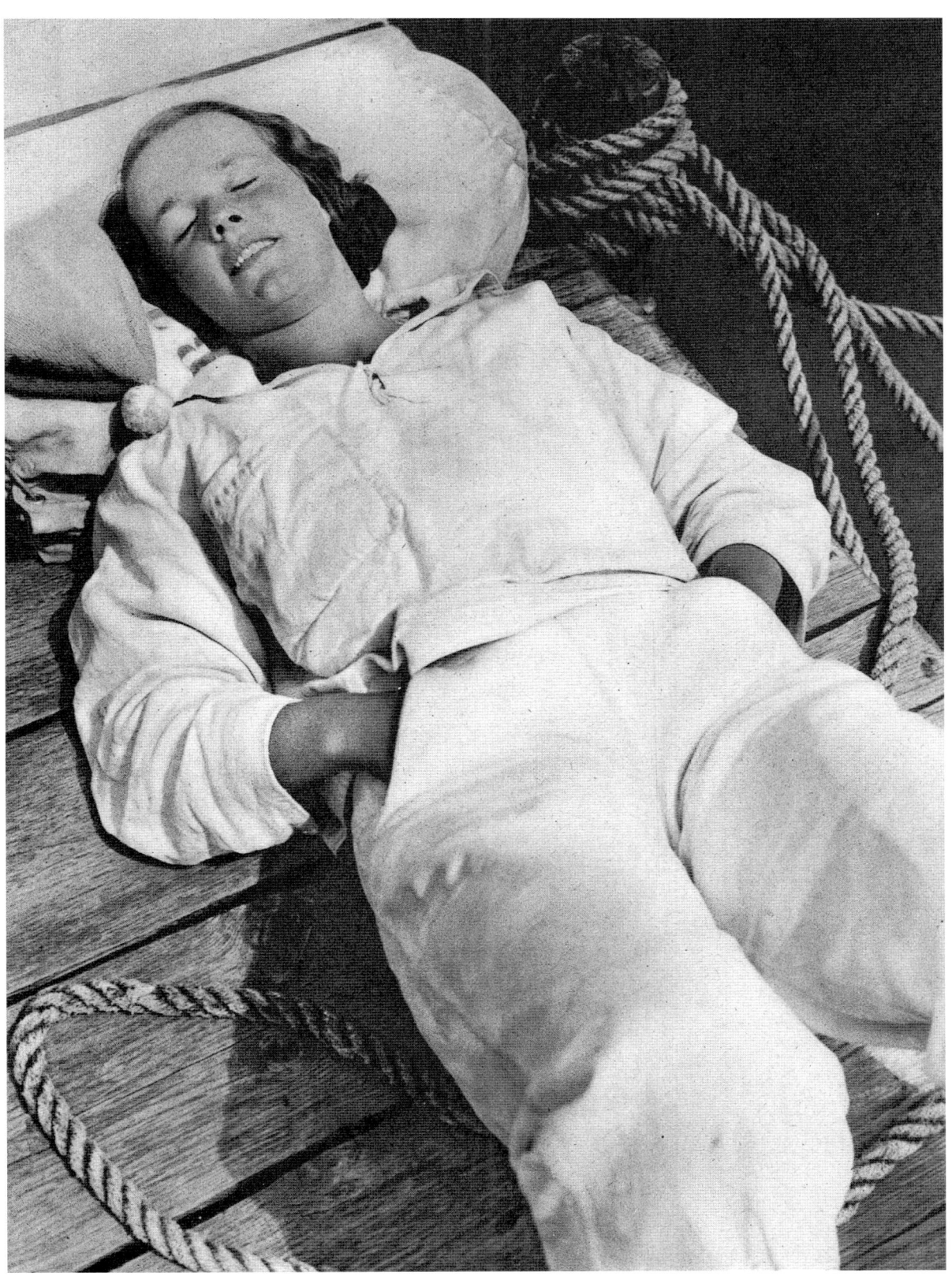

MOTHERS AND CHILDREN

also enjoy free recreation! Hundreds of thousands who live under unfavourable conditions in cities are sent to the country. Here they have an opportunity of gaining new strength and vigour at vacation homes or on the farm, while the costs are borne by the National Socialist People's Welfare Association.

CARE FOR THE HEREDITARILY HEALTHY

is the first duty of the National Socialist People's Welfare Association. The State provides for the unfit in Germany as in all other countries, but the National Socialist Reich also endeavours through its welfare work to protect and further the health of its racially and hereditarily sound children who are born of poor parents.

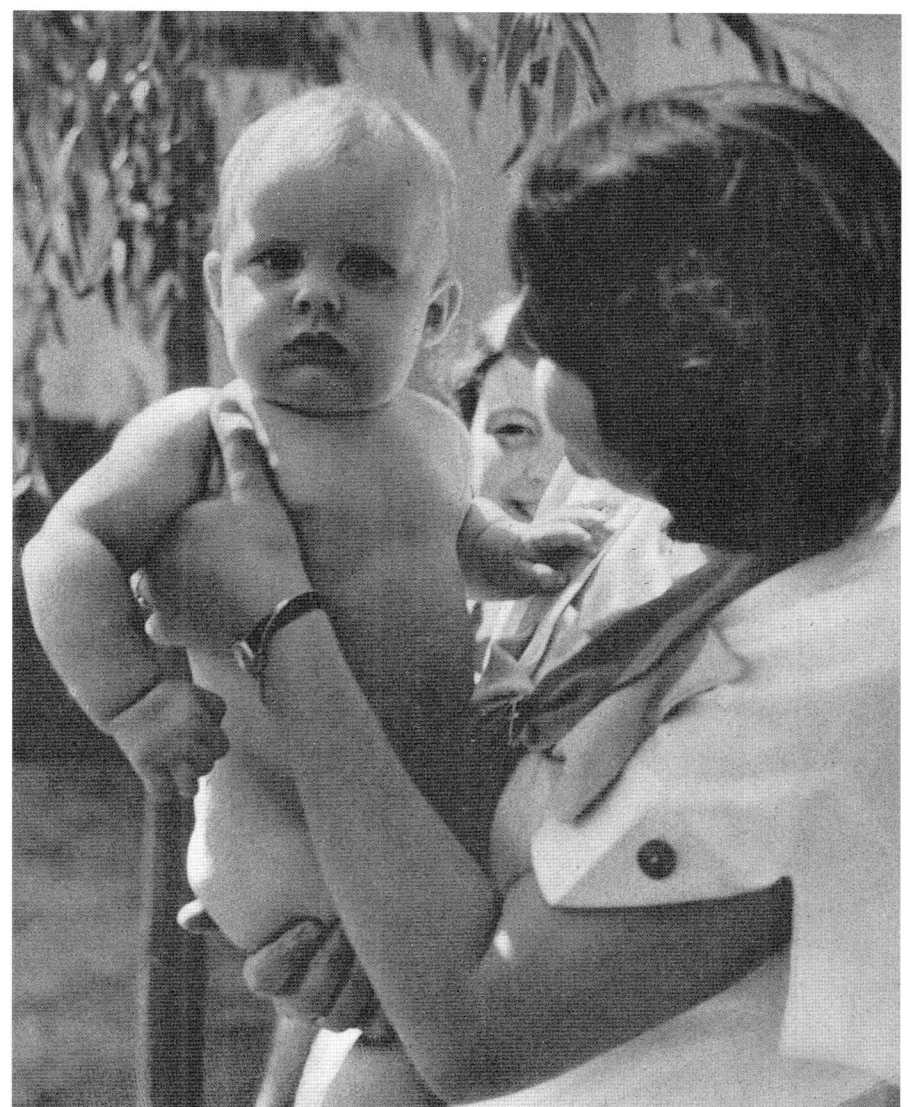

OUT OF HIS RETIREMENT

to collect for the Winter Relief Fund!

Over 300,000,000 marks are contributed annually by the German people in order that their less fortunate fellow beings may not go cold or hungry.

Less than 1% of this sum is spent for administrative purposes since most of the services are honorary.

The German film star, Jenny Jugo, officiates at a public soup kitchen.

EACH CONTRIBUTES

what he can. The Storm Troopers donate their youthful strength to the common cause, while grandmother fulfils her election obligation.

Thousands of invalids insisted on being conveyed to the polls in order to cast their votes.

Everything for Germany!

The Labour Service youth also assists in furthering the Winter Relief Work.

A HOHENZOLLERN PRINCE,

AUGUST WILHELM ("AUWI"),

IN THE RANKS OF THE FÜHRER

In Catholic Oberammergau the Passion player wears a brown shirt and swastika.

WHAT IS THE ATTITUDE OF THE FORMER "RED" WORKER TOWARDS NATIONAL COMRADESHIP?

On July 30th, 1936, the third birthday of the New Reich, I made a photographic tour of a Berlin district over which the Communist flag once waved. The pictures reproduced on the following pages are typical of what I saw.

NATIONAL..

A "Hotbed of Communism", where the streets were once filled with the barricades of the Red Front, observes the third anniversary of the New Reich. The flags are still red, but instead of the sickle and hammer they now display the swastika. Thus is celebrated the rise to power of Communism's greatest enemy.

COMMUNITY

The exclusive Hasenheide district of Berlin
exhibits the same flags — the same attitude

The Saar: 90 % for Hitler Germany

FORCED JOY?

The international press has informed its readers that the German people are forced to follow the Hitler banner, but the information of the press is not always correct. Shortly before the Saar election, for example, most of the foreign newspapers assured their readers that the inhabitants of the Saar were definitely against union with National Socialist Germany. The picture above, which was taken immediately after the election, depicts the spirit which prevailed. Below: A street in the Free City of Danzig during the last election campaign.

The Free City of Danzig: 60 % pure "Nazi"

"BLOOD AND SOIL"

If this idea, this fundamental principle of National Socialism could be described in word and picture, such a description would fill the greater part of this book, for Germany's whole future depends on it, and not only Germany's. "Blood and Soil" signifies a universal philosophy without which no people can assert itself for long in the history of civilization.

For centuries the intellectual forces of Europe have been concentrating themselves more and more in the cities, and for this reason the municipal populations have gained preeminence in the life of the nation, utilizing their gradually acquired power for exploiting the rural population. This tendency has resulted generally in a declining peasantry. In America, plans are being drawn up for assisting the farmers through emergency measures, but Germany is attacking this problem through a fundamental recognition of rural life.

In reality, the cities are little more than parasitic growths, since they draw their entire nourishment from the land of the peasant. Moreover, the life-blood of the city is also derived from this source. The metropolis with its unfavourable conditions for children is not even able to maintain its own population. If Berlin, for example, were forced to rely upon its own birth-rate, it would shrink within five generations from its present 4,000,000 inhabitants to a mere 100,000.

THE LIFE OF A NATION IS ROOTED IN ITS SOIL

Instead of ignoring him, the Third Reich concedes the peasant a foremost position, this interest in the rural populace being expressed in three important measures: the Hereditary Estate Law, market regulation, and new settlement of the land.

The Hereditary Estate Law guarantees the permanence of the farms. Never again can a German farm be auctioned off because of debts nor can it be dismantled or divided for lack of money. The eternal soil shall belong to the eternal source of life.

The market regulation establishes a control over the prices and distribution of farm products. Firmly established prices throughout the year for the principal products exclude speculation and at the same time guarantee existence in the city and on the farm. The price levels are established upon the basis of the vital necessities of agriculture, and for this reason as well as because of increased production, the total income of agriculture has increased almost 50%.

New settlements are made possible through the acquisition of new land (Labour Service) and through the partitioning of larger estates. Thousands of German families are thus returned to their own land each year.

Through the "production campaign", which has been rigorously carried out in the Third Reich, the production of the German soil is now able to nourish 90% instead of 60% of the population. And this campaign is progressing because the German nation is determined to provide adequate nourishment for its own people. It is not envious of the land of its neighbours because it does not require additional territory.

GERMANY HAS RETURNED TO HER OWN SOIL

Where once the flags of anti-peasant Communism heralded an attempt to conquer Germany (see page 36), Berlin today celebrates a rural
HARVEST THANKSGIVING FESTIVAL

The Reverse Side

Study this stretch of the National Motor Highway carefully.

Observe how it passes directly through the cultivated fields, requiring that the entire system of farming be revised.

It is true that the peasants were compensated for any losses incurred through this construction project, but the unavoidable disturbance of life-long peasant customs and habits cannot be remedied so easily.

In this case, the individual must make a sacrifice for the nation as a whole.

THIS PICTURE IS SYMBOLIC —

The National Motor Highway represents the common interests, the cultivated fields, the private interests in the new State.

As in every great revival, every revolutionary epoch, the interests of individuals are sometimes infringed upon.

To reorganize requires sacrifices, this being the price of the advantages to be obtained.

In the beginning it is always a few revolutionary spirits who wish to bring about a change, who are willing to sacrifice and who have a vision of the future advantages. If they succeed, they become the creators of a new epoch. Opposed to them are those who object to any change in the status quo, or in other words, the critics. These two groups are known in Germany today as the National Socialists and the "Meckerer" (grumblers).

Naturally, the "Meckerer" is always in the right since "right" is in every case on the side of the traditional, the customary. National Socialism, however, intends to create a new conception of "right", which of course will appear "wrong" to the creature of habit.

It is futile to dispute "right" and "wrong" because during an age of revolution deeds alone are decisive, and even these can be judged only in the light of later history.

There is also another aspect. Up until now I have painted an entirely favourable picture of the activities and endeavours in the New Germany. I have represented the national situation as though this complete reorganization must have meant increased happiness to everyone. One thing, however, is lacking in such a picture — the sacrifice made by the nation, the sacrifice of the individual in favour of the community and the present-day sacrifice of the community for the welfare of future generations.

Tragedy is also involved in the present development of Germany, and this tragedy cannot be simply ignored. On the contrary, it must be considered and dealt with.

Let us take the example of the peasant whose farm is traversed by the National Motor Highway. If he is a National Socialist, he endures this sacrifice for the good of the community, but if he belongs to the opposition, he makes the sacrifice nevertheless, although in the latter case he has the feeling that he is being imposed on personally. He thus gives vent to his feelings through . . . "Meckerei".

It has always been so in the world. Those who sacrifice willingly belong to the creators, and thereby enjoy an exalted feeling of having shared in the creation. Those who are forced to sacrifice, however, are the afflicted, the unfortunates. Considered from this point of view, it must be admitted that there are many who have been made unhappy by these new developments.

In this connection, I should like to make a personal observation. I realized after only a few weeks sojourn in the New Reich that the critics of the National Socialist Movement can be immediately recognized even before they have uttered a discontented word. Their political attitude is disclosed in their attitude towards life in general. If the person in question is disinterested, casual and reserved, he is certainly a "Meckerer" or at least a member of the political opposition. If, on the other hand, he is lively and daring, he is certainly an exponent of the Movement — he is a National Socialist.

I felt myself irresistibly drawn to this latter group, simply on the grounds of common interests.

I am nevertheless a critic among critics, and for this reason I can understand other kindred spirits. I observe at every hand things and conditions which should be changed — changed completely. At the same time, however, I perceive among the National Socialists men who are determined to bring about these alterations. That is the significance of the Movement — the will to improve.

For this reason, the Movement provides an unlimited field of activity for all constructive critics. If the country were stagnant, this creative urge would suffocate, but where everything is in movement, each has the opportunity of cooperating according to his abilities.

The task of reorganization requires endless cooperation and countless collaborators. That is the principle of leadership.

The new Movement does not desire a mass of helpless and constantly afflicted followers, but creators and leaders. From the Young People's Organization upward, every attempt is made to encourage the qualities of leadership, and whoever has been singled out by fate to play a part in the shaping of the present epoch will find a more fertile field for his endeavours in the New Germany than elsewhere.

There are naturally many who belong to that unfortunate group known as the professional critics and who thus attempt to influence their fellowmen. Their instrument is the typewriter. The activities of these "scribes" are circumvented to a certain extent by the system of censorship in the Third Reich, a condition which is often found to be unbearable — especially to professional critics in foreign countries.

I do not believe, however, that the suppression of this field of activity will represent an irreparable loss to Germany. I do not know of a single occasion when the vital history of the world was made by authors, since history is not words but deeds. The man of action may also lead in words, but these merely provide the inspiration to action.

Only he who is capable of transforming his criticism into deeds is worth heeding.

"Judea Declares War on Germany"

In the last German election, 99% of all those who enjoyed the franchise participated — a world record! Of these, 99% voted for the leadership of Adolf Hitler — another world record! In other words, 99% of Germany's voters signified their willingness to cooperate in the great work of revival. The 1% which refused its support consists of members of other races — principally Jews.

Never in the history of the world have the children of Israel been able to fit into a Nationalist State. They were the enemies of the mighty Empire of the Pharaohs because they would not submit to the customary labour service. They were even less popular in the Babylonian kingdom, and because of their constant uprisings the otherwise tolerant Ceasars finally decided to destroy Jerusalem and to scatter its populace in the four directions of the wind.

Today, with the development of the modern National State, the ancient Jewish problem again arises. The principles of leadership and those of Judea will clash as long as civilization endures. We are not concerned here with a judgment of values but with a historical fact.

Many nations, particularly America, evidence little understanding of this fact. The ideal behind the American democracy is to unite all of the people within the bonds of brotherhood and democracy.

This ideal, however, has little connection with practical life in America, for the United States actually lead the world in racial differentiation. Not even with a member of the yellow race will a white American enter into social intercourse, let alone with a Mexican or a negro. All of the darker races are strictly segregated, confined in their activities and treated with the utmost contempt. About 20,000,000 members of the American population are suppressed in this manner.

How much more considerate is Germany's treatment of her half million Jews! Their prospects are much more favourable than, for example, those of the Californian of Japanese descent, who is practically confined to vegetable gardening and hawking for a living. And no comparison is possible with the plight of the negro in the Southern States.

THE FAULT FINDERS

New Revelations

Nazi Atrocities

It is well known that the daily programme of the Nazis consists to a great extent of atrocities. Up to the present time, however, no one has been able to provide conclusive proof of this commonly accepted fact . . . . I succeeded, however, in tracking down several of these deeds, and the ensuing pictures will reveal conditions which are beyond human belief . . . .

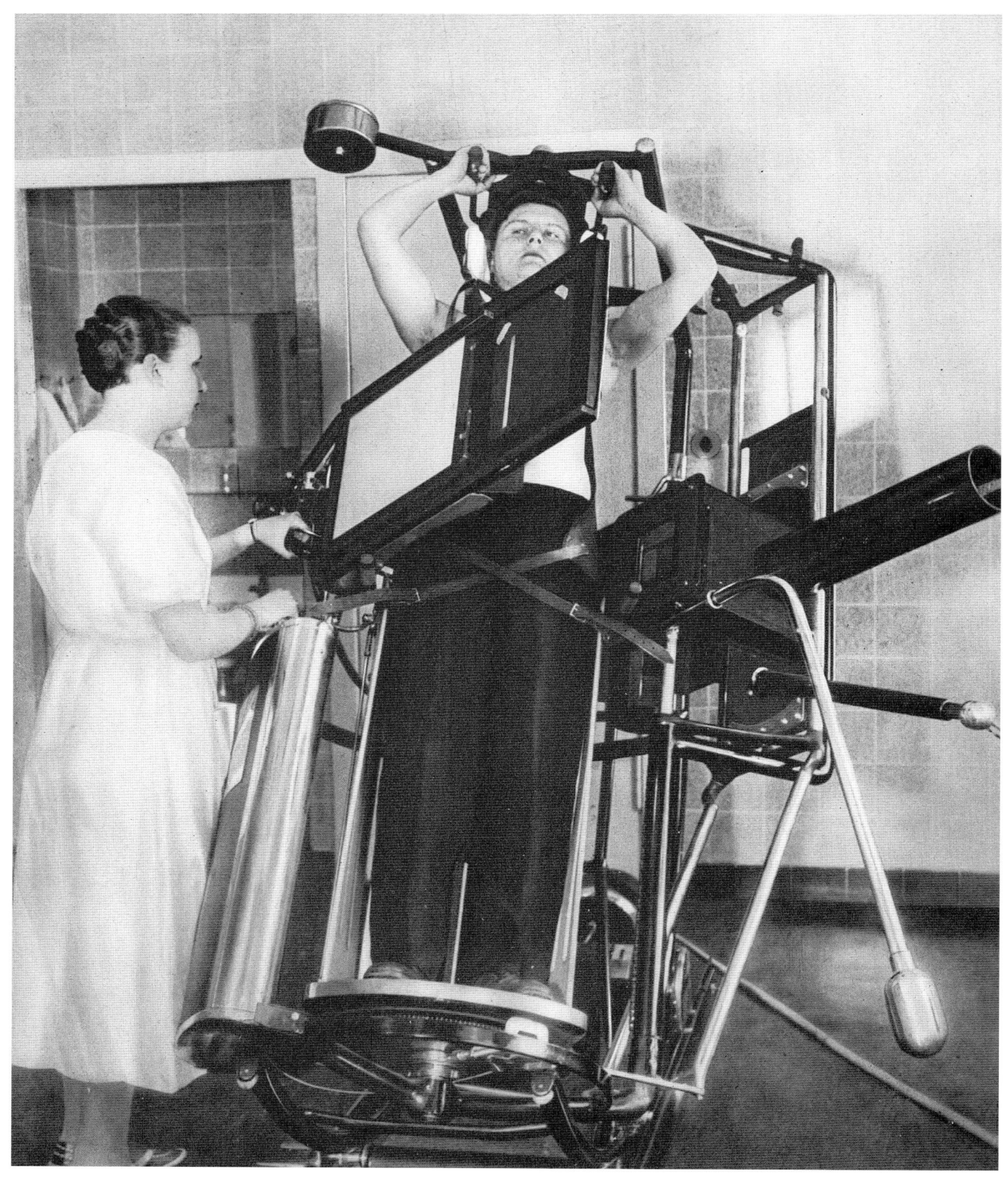

"A TWENTIETH CENTURY TORTURE CHAMBER"

"The victim of the Nazis is strapped into this horrible looking machine. Then, by means of mysterious rays invented by a German named Röntgen, his body is rendered totally transparent. Such methods are resorted to daily in every German hospital."

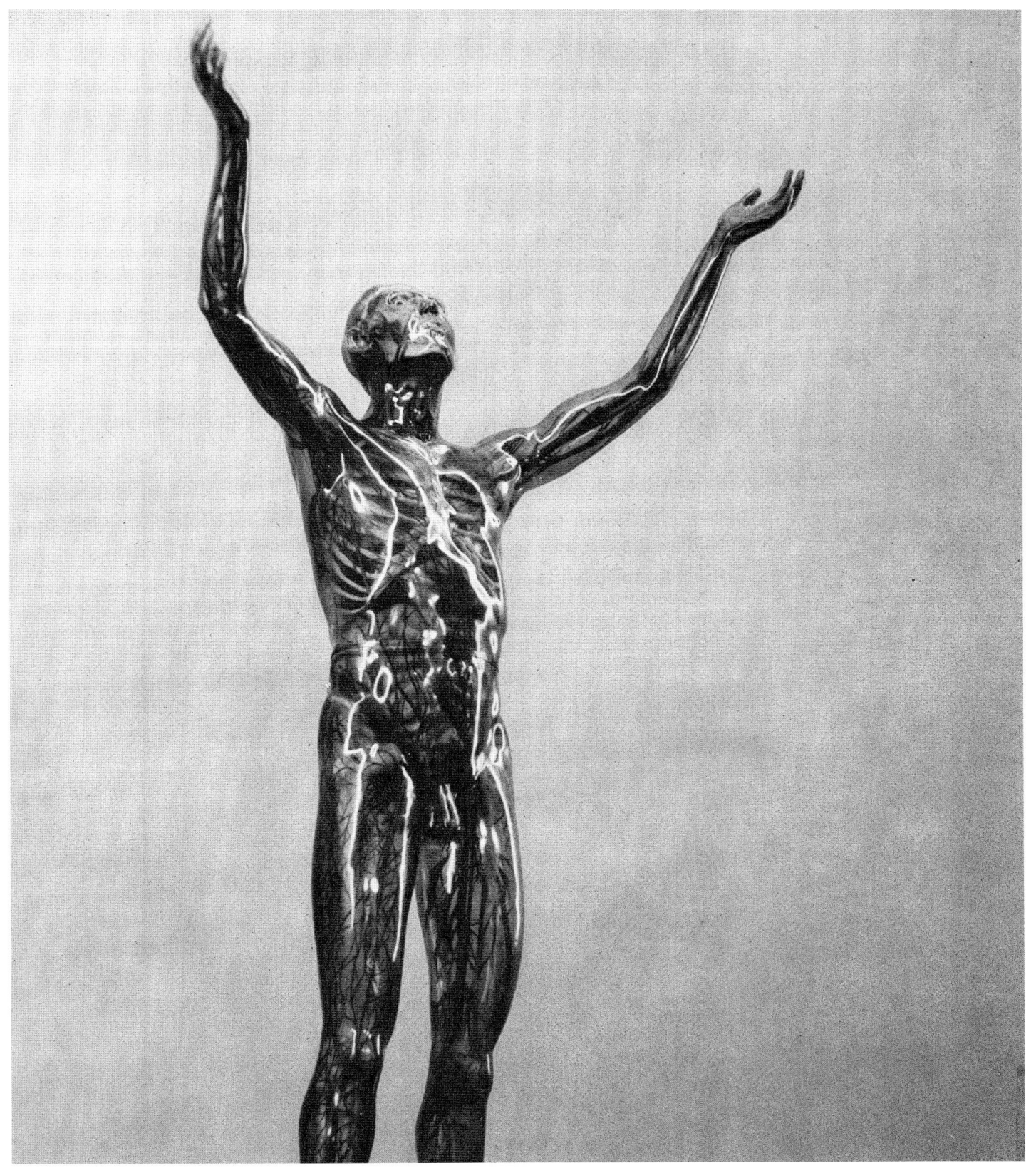

"THE VICTIM WHO HAS BECOME TRANSPARENT"

"From his positition one can see that during his last hour he begged for mercy — but in vain. His bones and organs have been shamelessly revealed, and still worse, the German Hygiene Museum in Dresden has placed him on public exhibition at the Paris World Fair of 1937."

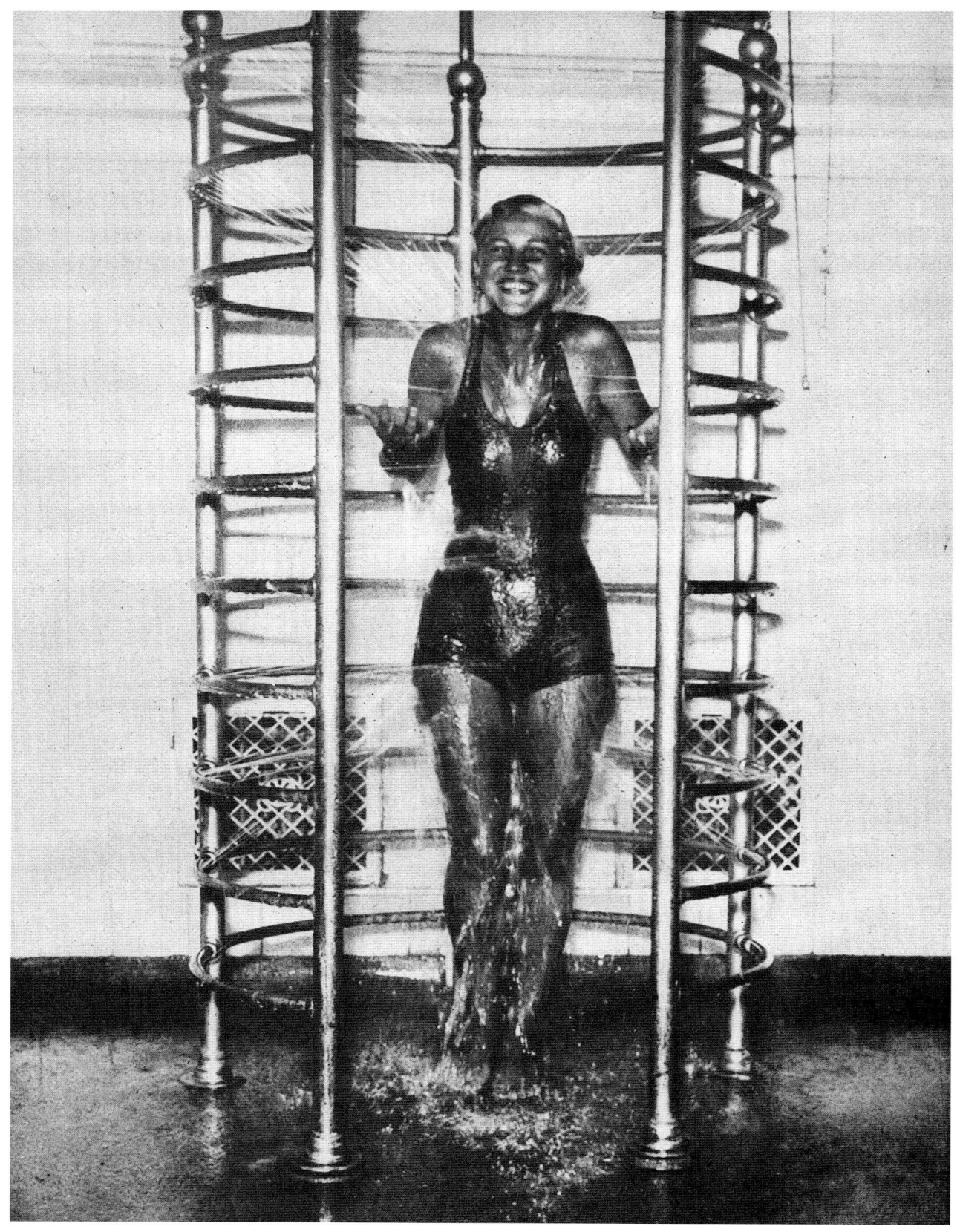

"NAZI TORTURE CAGE"

"One sees here how a harmless maiden is tortured. Needle-like jets of water are shot at her from all directions, and she is tickled in this manner until she laughs herself to death. This gruesome instrument has become an essential part of every public swimming bath."

"NAZI POISONING"

"The German people, especially the women, are being poisoned in a most heartless manner. A Nazi is here caught in the act of offering an innocent maiden an alcoholic drink. In connection with a special publicity week for German wine she and many other maidens are systematically 'infected'."

"NAZI SECRET AGENT"

"Dressed as a watch-maker, he wanders from town to town, but his scrutinizing glances reveal his true character. He is spying on incautious citizens, and if anyone is caught laughing, his future fate is indeed uncertain."

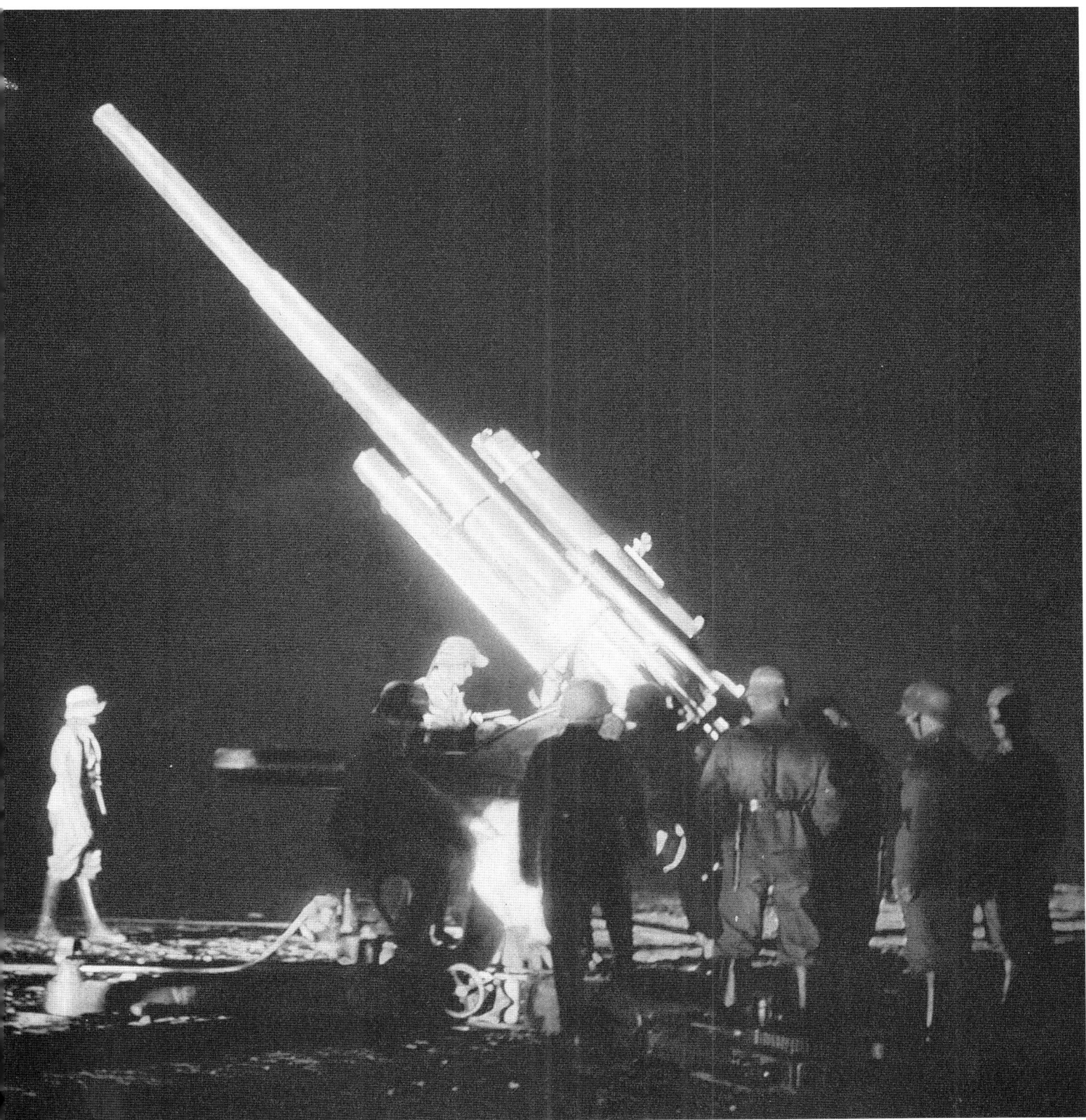

"AND NOW THE WORST OF ALL!"

"For some incomprehensible reason the Germans are determined not to permit foreign aviators to drop bombs on their heads, and, inspired by an inhuman desire for self-preservation, they have prepared in a most ruthless manner to exterminate this form of aviation sport."

"Los Angeles Times"* — September 15th, 1936

THE FÜHRER

in the eyes of the "democratic" world

* A typical American metropolitan newspaper of a conservative type

HITLER SAYS THAT GERMANY NEEDS THE RICH LANDS OF THE SOVIETS

Nuremberg, Sept. 12 (Associated Press). While hundreds of Nazi war planes thundered aggressively in the air, Adolf Hitler declared today that Germany would enjoy an undreamt of prosperity if she only possessed the rich agricultural lands and mineral-laden mountains of Soviet Russia. In a speech before the Labour Front, following his assurances to thousands of worshipping young boys and girls that Germany would triumph over Russia "when the hour strikes", the Führer shouted:

"If I had the Urals, if we possessed Siberia, if we had the Ukraine — National Socialist Germany would swim in abundance!"

Such was the tone in the American press on September 12th, 1936 of the reports on the National Socialist Party Congress in Nuremberg. The stories on the following day were even worse:

"GERMANY READY FOR WAR SAYS HITLER"

appeared in large headlines.

Then came the popular American weekly news magazines with their sensational reports. "Time", the leading publication of this type, made the following statements:

"On a podium high as a church tower, with clashing military bands, ceremonious singing, machine-like marching in goose-step and dramatic torchlight effects, Adolf Hitler was represented more than ever as that which he in reality is — the Teutonic Messiah. His message this year was more audacious than ever before. At the moment when excitement had reached its zenith, 400 new German heavy bombing and pursuit planes of all types suddenly appeared, and literally darkened the sky above Nuremberg. The thunder of their motors made the windows rattle and the hearts of the Germans swell. Then while every radio station in Germany broadcast his words and every German was ordered to listen, while loud speakers in the streets and squares of every German city, town and village trumpeted, Adolf Hitler declared with breath-taking simplicity: "If I had the Ural Mountains, if we possessed Siberia, if we had the Ukraine, then Nazi Germany would swim in prosperity ... Let Russia exhibit her Soviet star. We shall win under the sign of the swastika!"

It was obvious that Germany was planning a campaign of conquest against Russia. Sidelights reveal most effectively the general attitude which developed as a result of these outbursts. The conservative "Los Angeles Times" published the following statement in connection with a book review:

"Now that Hitler is shouting what he would do if he had parts of Russia and France, when Germans as well as Italians are supporting the Spanish rebels with guns, aeroplanes, money and men, all that is written about Hitler and his unfortunate country deserves our attention ... This book delves into the background of National Socialism's rise to power and describes the secret forces which are at work to abolish Hitler and to restrain Germany in her headlong rush behind the wild man of Europe into a new and still more devastating war."

Russia's representative, Litvinoff, could thus calmly declare before the League of Nations that the gates of Geneva should be closed to a land which openly declares its intentions "of annexing by force extensive territories belonging to other countries". Other similar reports, all of them direct from Moscow, were circulated throughout the world by the outstanding news agencies.

BUT WHAT DID THE FÜHRER **REALLY** SAY?

His address dealt principally with the execution of his new Four Year Plan and the synthetic production of important raw materials. It was held before members of the Labour Service in the sober Nuremberg Congress Hall. I was present on this occasion, in the press box. There was naturally no trace of the breath-taking theatrical display of which "Time", for example, speaks. The speech was disturbed on one occasion by the accidental crossing of several aeroplanes, but that was long before the Führer came to speak about Russia. His statements in this connection are reproduced here just as I received them from the Reich Broadcasting Company where they were transcribed from the original recording:

"The world was not created in a single day, nor did the nations come into being in a single year. All of this required time. The deciding factor is, however, that we should not believe that this process can be accelerated if we for the time being destroy everything ... I prefer to take another course, clarify conceptions, abolish antagonisms and slowly achieve unity through training. I do not intend to produce chaos in order to be able to say 18 years later, 'Since we began with chaos, we naturally cannot be expected to have recovered completely'. I will begin with order as the foundation for the revival.

"We must do it that way since I am not in the fortunate position of the Soviet Jews. Had I eighteen times as much ground, how much do you think we should then produce? ... These incapable leaders are not able to rescue their people from distress although they are literally swimming in superfluous land. What blockheads they are! (Laughter and applause) ...

"You may be assured that if I had the Urals with their unlimited deposits of raw materials, if we possessed Siberia with its endless forests, if we had the Ukraine with its rolling grain fields, Germany under National Socialist leadership would swim in abundance. We should produce, and the individual German would find his place in life. It is more difficult for us despite the poverty of our soil, our limited territory and our scarcity of raw materials, to develop a form of life which is higher than that existing in this Bolshevist paradise of Soviet Russia.

"No, my friends; our lot is not an easy one. But do not believe that I am complaining or despairing. On the contrary, I find it wonderful that fate devises great tasks for men and ages. I do not know the word, 'impossible'! You may say, 'That is impossible. What is impossible? Everything is possible when there is a will! (Thunderous applause).

"Courage is naturally necessary as well as energy, resolution and a firm belief. I can assure everyone of this. How much faith do you think was necessary 18 years ago when I founded the Party, and what degree of courage did I require to carry on an individual combat against a whole world of preconceptions and opponents? Do you believe that it was easier then than today when I tell you that within the next year and a half we must have relieved this and that distress, or that within four years we must have solved these and those problems? All of this appears to me to be easier than it did formerly when I began, as a lonesome wanderer, the path that was to lead from nothing at all to the leadership of the German nation . . ."

<u>The Führer actually proclaimed exactly the contrary to that which the headlines in the international press asserted, namely, that Germany, lacking the unlimited natural resources which were at the disposal of the incapable Bolshevists, must carry out her new Four Year Plan by means of substitute materials produced by complicated methods.</u>

Why does the foreign press raise such an outcry at every event which transpires in Germany? A typical explanation of this can be gained from the highly reputed, genuinely Anglo-Saxon "Review of Reviews", which in its August, 1936 issue prints the results of a special ballot showing the consensus of opinion on the part of its readers regarding the question: 'In the case of a war between Germany and Russia, which side would you favour?' The result was two to one for Russia. And this among intelligent readers of the upper 'bourgeoisie'! The editor appended the following statement:

"The majority of these typical Americans are of the opinion that Russia is intent on the development of her own country through the Five Year Plan and new democratic constitution, while Germany, in a condition of dangerous agitation, fosters plans as in 1914 for the conquest of foreign territories. The question put before the readers was whether they preferred the plough or the sword; it was one of humanitarian values."

The true significance of these statements lies in the fact that they indicate the unbelievable success of Soviet propaganda in America.

THE ATTITUDE OF THE WORLD TOWARDS GERMANY WILL CHANGE AS SOON AS IT REALIZES THAT A NEW SYSTEM OF ORDER IS DEVELOPING HERE IN THE MIDST OF THE GROWING BOLSHEVIST-DEMOCRATIC CHAOS.

In the face of fratricide and church burning in Spain, threatening raised fists in France and Red disorders throughout the world, this work is designed to further Germany's point of view.

". . . I prefer to take another course, clarify conceptions, abolish antagonisms and slowly achieve unity through training." The Führer on September 12th, 1936 before the Labour Front

An Opinion by Lloyd George

from an article in the "Daily Express", London, following his German tour in September, 1936

"I have just met the German Führer and learned something of the great changes he has brought about. Whatever one may think of his methods — and they are certainly not those of a parliamentarian country — there can nevertheless be no doubt that he has brought about a remarkable revolution in the spirit of the Germans, in their relations with one another and in their social and economic attitude. He was justified in declaring at Nuremberg that his Movement has made a new Germany. It is no longer the Germany of the first 10 post-war years — crushed, defeated and weighed down by a feeling of sorrow and incapability, but a Germany full of hope and confidence, and inspired by a new resolution.

"One man performed this miracle. He is a born leader, a magnetic, dymamic personality with a common aim, a resolute will and a fearless heart.

"He is the national leader not only in name but also in deeds. He has protected his people against the potential enemies surrounding them, and he has secured them against the constant fear of starvation which remained as one of the most tenacious memories of the final war years and the early period of peace. During these dark years, over 700,000 died of hunger. Regarding his popularity, especially among the youth, there cannot be the slightest doubt. The older people have faith in him and the youth idolizes him. It is not a question of admiration for a popular leader, but veneration of a national hero who has rescued his country from despair and humiliation.

"**Hitler is the George Washington of Germany,** the man who made his country independent of all of its oppressors. To those who have not actually seen and experienced the manner in which Hitler rules over the hearts and spirits of the German people this description may seem exaggerated, but it is nevertheless the plain truth. This whole nation will work better, make greater sacrifices, and if necessary, fight with firmer resolution because Hitler demands it.

"On the other hand, those who maintain that Germany has returned to her old imperialistic temperament can have no understanding for the character of the change.

"**What Hitler said in Nuremberg is true. The Germans would resist to the last man any attempt to invade their country. But they have no desire to march into any other country. The leaders of the new Germany realize too well that Europe is too important a matter to be overrun and violated by any single nation, regardless of the size of its armaments.**

"That Germany is rearming cannot be denied. After all the victors in the Great War except England disregarded their own disarmament pledges, the Führer abrogated the agreement which bound his own country, thus following the example of he nations who were responsible for the Versailles Treaty. It is today a commonly admitted part of Hitler's policy to develop an army strong enough to resist any attack, regardless of from which side it may come. I believe that he has already reached this point of inviolability.

"Any attempt to repeat Poincaré's methods in the Ruhr District would meet with the fanatical opposition of thousands of men who do not regard death or the Fatherland as a sacrifice but as an honour.

"Catholics and Protestants, Prussians and Bavarians, employers and employees have all been welded into a unified nation. Religious, provincial and class distinctions no longer divide the country. A passionate spirit of unity prevails, born of dire necessity.

"I encountered throughout Germany a strong and uncompromising enmity for Bolshevism combined with a genuine admiration for the British people and the sincere desire for a better and friendlier understanding with England."

The Heart of Europe

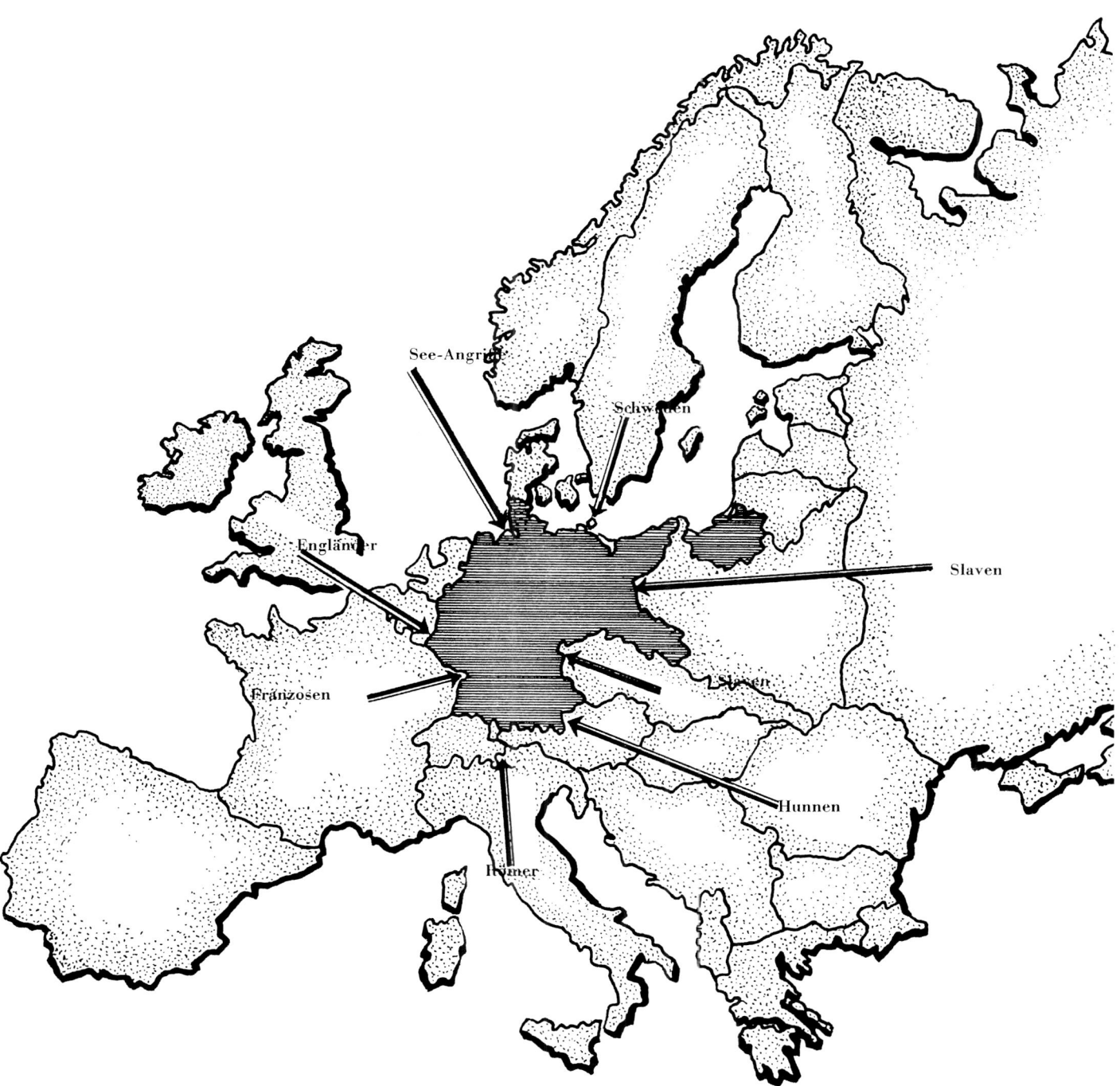

The above picture illustrates the manner in which "wild" Germans attacked "mild" Romans. This battle took place in the Teutoburg Forest nineteen hundred years ago. The Romans had come to subjugate the German people and introduce Latin civilization. But the Germans did not appreciate these intentions, preferring rather to develop their own culture according to their individual nature.

And just as they repulsed the Romans, they have defended their country in the heart of Europe again and again throughout the centuries. Since the earliest times the Germans have resisted the constant pressure of the masses from the East. They fought for centuries with the Asiatic Huns, they drove the Turks from the gates of Europe, and even today they must resist the pressure from the Slavic East.

Two centuries ago Germany was the constant battlefield of Europe for a period of 30 years. The French, Spaniards, Swedes and Poles invaded and devastated the entire country, giving rise to the tragedy of disintegration.

A contemporary description depicts the true horrors of this period:

"No words are heard other than 'Kill! Thrust! Strike! Stab! Spare none!' Every street and alley flows with blood, and whole houses are full of corpses and lamenting people. The husband is stabbed in the arms of his wife, and the wife is dragged from the side of her husband by the barbarous enemy. One sees nothing but the plundering of houses and annihilation of farms. In fact, everything must be cleaned out, swept away. Everything must be torn, ruined, violated."

The Thirty Years' War cost Germany half of her population. But scarcely had the children of this period of horror reached maturity than the French again appeared on expeditions of plunder and destruction.

While France was basking in the brilliance of her "Roi Soleil" Germany was a poverty-stricken, oppressed country. It was not until the time of her famous leader, Frederick the Great, that she was again able to assert herself.

In the West . . .   The National War Memorial

GERMANY'S TWO LARGEST MONUMENTS . . . . . .

At the beginning of the eighteenth century Germany was again turned into the battlefield of Europe by Napoleon, and many are still living who remember the last time that France declared war on Germany.

And then the WORLD WAR . . .

Who bears the "guilt"?

Mankind — and the German accepts his responsibility with every other.

It is not "guilt" and "innocence" which are significant in the life of mankind, but facts alone.

The fact is that Germany, as the HEART OF EUROPE, is in the most dangerous position of any country in Europe.

Tannenberg Memorial ... In the East

.... STERN REMINDERS OF ENEMY INVASIONS

Neither in the West nor in the East does Germany possess natural protective frontiers. She lies like a nut in a nut-cracker. And the world should not wonder that the nut endeavours to defend itself.

But one can certainly live at peace with good neighbours. This fact is well realized, since Germany could never hope to gain any permanent advantage from a war, and could only protect what she already owns.

There is a neighbour in the East, however, the mightiest of all, who is preparing for international conquest . . . and this in the name of the Proletariat of the world.

This principle is merely a modern means of camouflaging a primaeval fact, the

ETERNAL SURGING OF THE RESTLESS EASTERN MASSES TOWARDS THE WEST!

THEREFORE ....

GERMANY MUST GUARD AND DEFEND

PEACE ON EARTH. This is the Christmas message. And in no other part of the world is it so deeply revered as in Germany.

PEACE ON EARTH. Not with League of Nations covenants, sanctions or agreements can the spirit of this message be apprehended, nor through any creation of agitated mankind.

PEACE ON EARTH is reborn and fostered only through the eternal recurrence of new life. The Christmas message is disseminated mildly from the cradle of each new-born child.

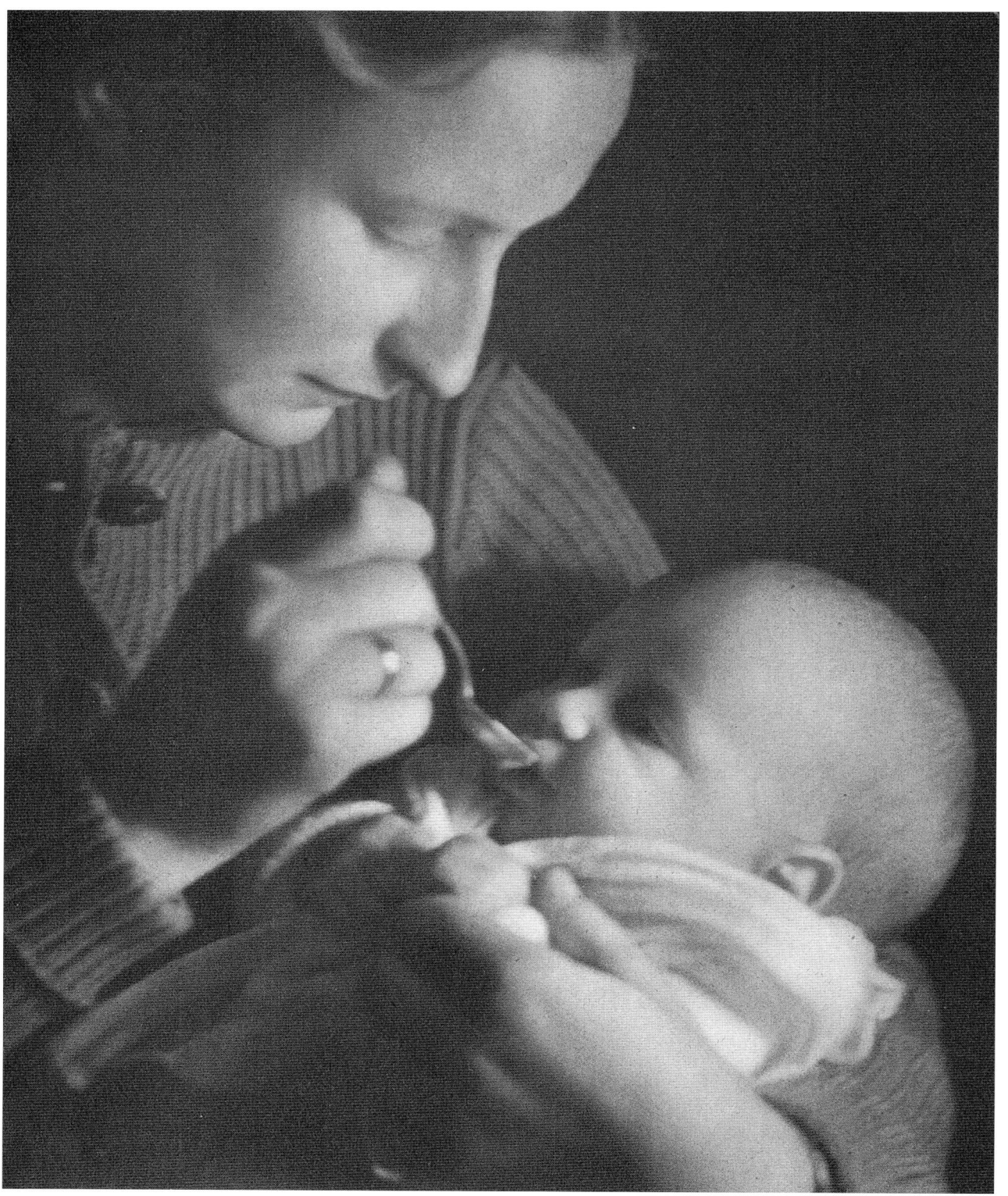

COUNTRY FOLK

TOWN FOLK

TYPICAL...

THE FORMER
Marxist-Jewish
Berlin Chief of Police,
GRESZINSKI

THE NEW
National Socialist
Chief of Police,
COUNT
HELLDORF

... CONTRASTS

THE RED

"Saviour" of Munich,

KURT EISNER

THE BROWN

Deliverer

of Bavaria,

RITTER VON EPP

In Berlin's formerly notorious "El Dorado",
a night-club for Lesbian women and feminine men

PROHIBITED

in the Third Reich

A Bavarian Wedding

As it is desired
in the
New Reich

Workers of the Krupp Firm respond enthusiastically to a campaign speech by the Führer

THE FÜHRER SPEAKS

The "Netherlands Hymn of Thanksgiving" is sung during the Führer's address in Cologne

"WE ASSEMBLE FOR PRAYER BEFORE GOD THE JUST . . . . ."

Tantum ergo...

RECRUIT

REKRUT

LABOUR SERVICE YOUTH

ARBEITSDIENSTMANN

OLYMPIASIEGERIN

Eager Spectators at the CHILDREN'S THEATRE

Grimm MÄRCHEN-Spiel

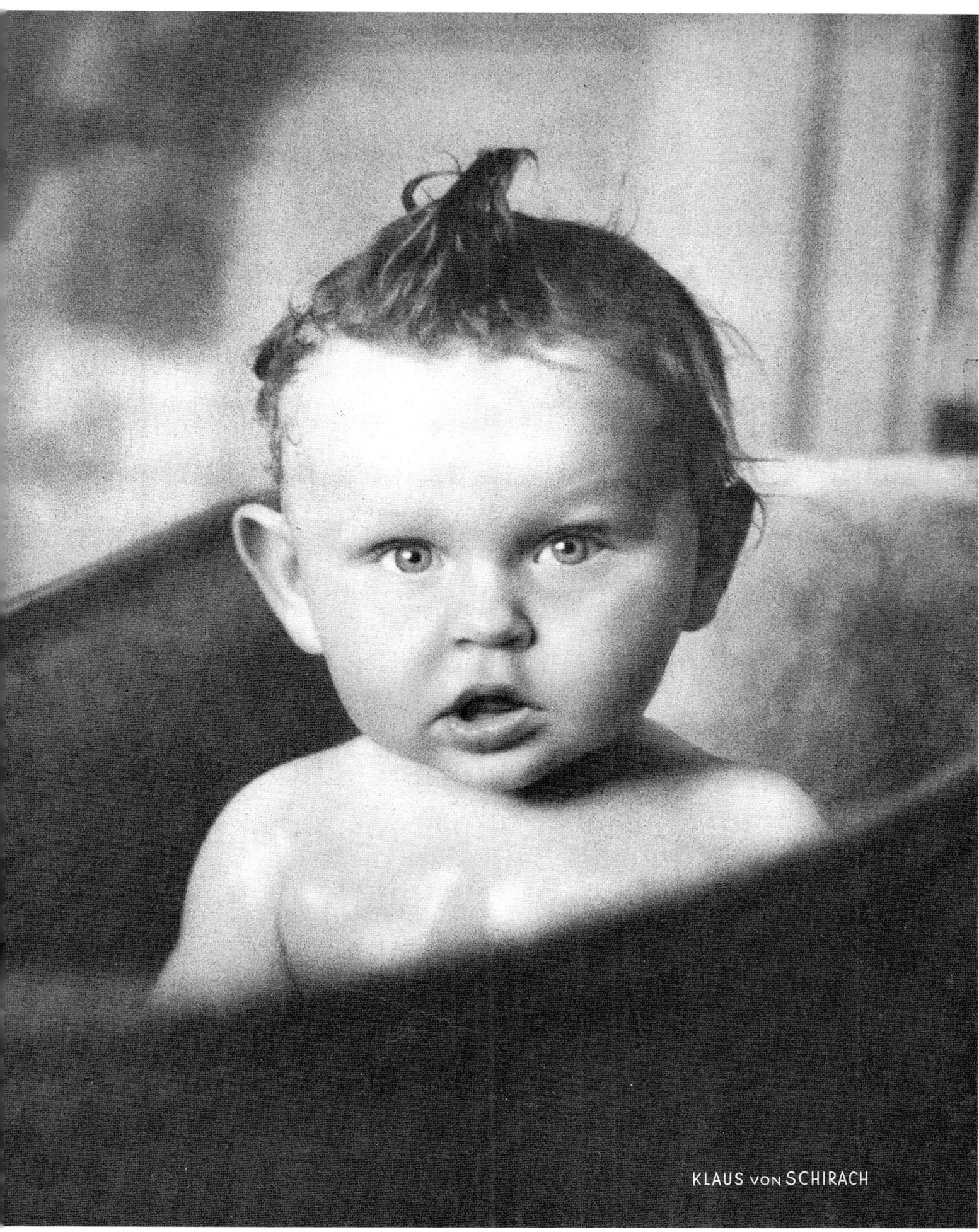
KLAUS von SCHIRACH

German Children — Children of Eve

A HAND TO THE FÜHRER....

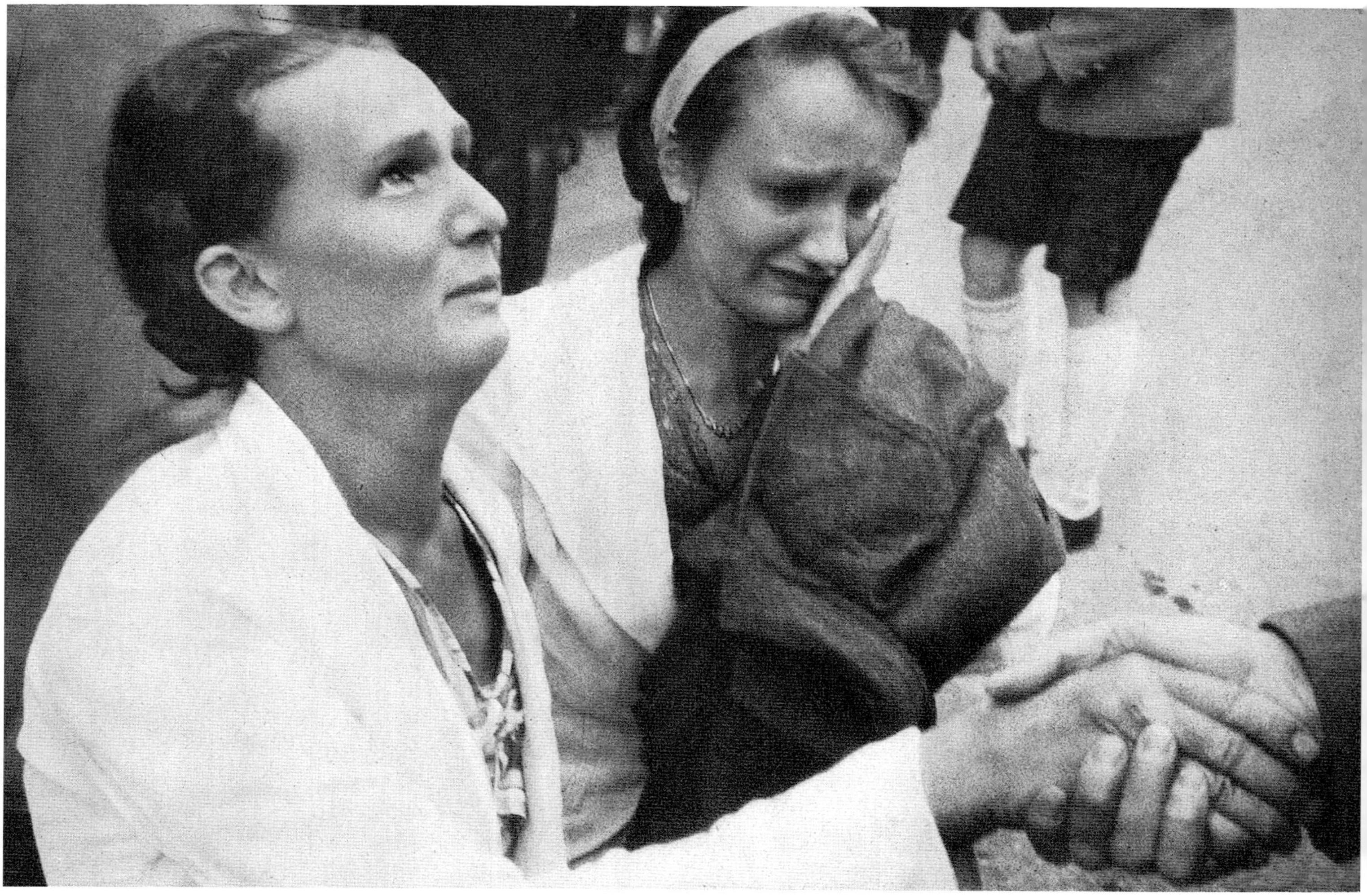

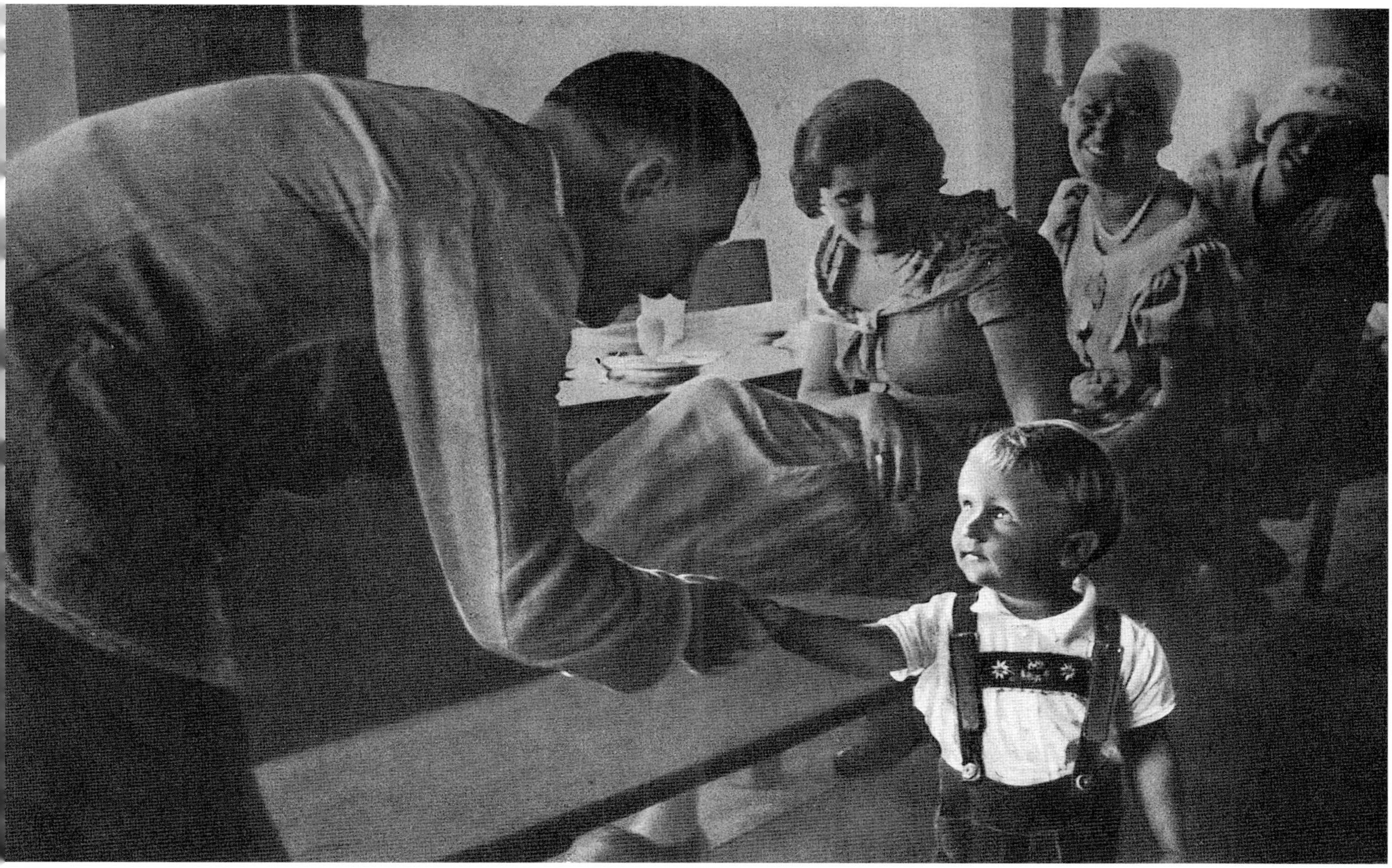

The greatest thing about him is not that he is our Führer,
And the hero of countless thousands,
But himself — straightforward, firm and unpretentious.

He controls the cords of all our actions,
And his spirit reaches to the stars;
But yet he remains a man — like you and me . . .

BALDUR VON SCHIRACH

Aller Welt die Hand...

A Hand Extended to All...

HELGA GOEBBELS